Portland Community College Libraries

WITHDRAWN

A HANDBOOK OF SHORT-TERM PSYCHODYNAMIC PSYCHOTHERAPY

D0222798

A HANDBOOK OF SHORT-TERM PSYCHODYNAMIC PSYCHOTHERAPY

Penny Rawson

KARNAC
LONDON   NEW YORK

First published in 2005 by
H. Karnac (Books) Ltd.
6 Pembroke Buildings, London NW10 6RE

Copyright © 2005 Penny Rawson

The right of Penny Rawson to be identified as the author of
this work has been asserted in accordance with §§ 77 and 78
of the Copyright Design and Patents Act 1988.

All rights reserved. No part of this publication may be repro-
duced, stored in a retrieval system, or transmitted, in any
form or by any means, electronic, mechanical, photocopying,
recording, or otherwise, without the prior written permission
of the publisher.

British Library Cataloguing in Publication Data

A C.I.P. for this book is available from the British Library

ISBN: 1 85575 304 9

Edited, designed and produced by The Studio Publishing
Services Ltd, Exeter EX4 8JN

Printed in Great Britain by Hobbs the Printers Ltd, Totton, Hampshire

10 9 8 7 6 5 4 3 2 1

www.karnacbooks.com

Contents

This book is dedicated to the late Louis Marteau who introduced me to the method of brief psychodynamic psychotherapy.

ACKNOWLEDGEMENTS

I would like to thank those who have assisted me in compiling this book. I am grateful to those clients who have permitted me to use material from their situations, using a pseudonym. I have amalgamated some of the clinical examples for confidentiality and all names are fictitious; any resemblance to an individual is therefore chance. I am indebted to Fr Tom, who has read, encouraged, and supported this work, and to Terry Baker, who has also proof read for me. I will always remember with gratitude the late Louis Marteau, who taught me so much about this brief method of psychodynamic psychotherapy.

Also thanks are due to Karnac for publishing this, my third book.

ABOUT THE AUTHOR

Dr Penny Rawson has published articles in various journals and has done a great deal of research into her specialism, brief psychodynamic psychotherapy. She is the author of *Short-Term Psychodynamic Psychotherapy: An Analysis of Key Principles*, which could be seen as the text book to accompany this basic guide to the practice of brief therapy. She has also written *Grappling with Grief*, which has been described as a book that normalizes grief.

She is the Director of *FASTPACE*, a consultancy specializing in brief pschodynamic therapy, training and supervision.

She adopted the acronym *FASTPACE* as her trade name. This seems an apt title for a therapy that is intended to work at a fast pace. The letters actually stand for Focal and Short Term Psychotherapy and Counselling Education. She has served on a number of national committees, including the British Association of Counselling and Psychotherapy's (BACP) Accreditation and Standards and Ethics. She has worked as a therapist for many years, managing services in higher education, as director of a youth counselling service and as partner of one of the first employee assistance programmes (EAPs) in the country.

INTRODUCTION

Why the book?

This book has been written in response to the interest shown in the short-term approach. Very many health authorities and doctors' surgeries now work predominantly in the brief approach, as do most university counsellors. The profession has begun to offer an increasing number of courses in various forms of brief work. Professionals are seeking to increase their knowledge of short-term therapy with a view to practising it, teaching it, or supervising others who are now working in this way.

Who the book is for

This book focuses on the basics for working in short-term psychodynamic psychotherapy. It is aimed primarily at the experienced therapist. The basic tenets of counselling and therapy are therefore assumed to be part of counsellors' existing repertoire of skills. This book might also be useful to any other therapist, supervisor, or trainer who wants to think about the basics of brief psychodynamic psychotherapy.

Additionally, this book will provide the lay person who is interested in knowing a little more about the brief approach with an outline of the method. In fact, many people are using aspects of counselling and therapy in their day to day dealings with others. The counselling continuum (see p. xviii) indicates the different levels of therapy and counselling that are appropriate for different issues. The recipient's expectations and needs are perhaps what define the role. For example, if someone visits the doctor, he or she may well apply counselling skills but the recipient of this does not perceive the doctor to be a counsellor or therapist. Friends share and help each other with their problems but do not call themselves counsellors or therapists. Some of the ideas in this book can usefully be taken on board not just by therapists. Having said that, I want to stress that the method of brief psychotherapy outlined here is a psychodynamic approach and in its entirety is best handled by the trained and supervised therapist. I use the terms psychodynamic counselling and psychotherapy interchangeably.

Many supervisors who have not trained specifically in the brief approach find themselves with supervisees who are practising in this way because their workplace demands it. This book will be useful for them to dip into from time to time, especially as it describes the brief approach as a treatment of choice.

Since this book has been based on a series of lectures, it may prove particularly useful for those therapists who want to train others in the brief approach. This might be as a specific training course, or it might be in the process of a training supervision.

The quick reference notes, articles and letters with reference to issues of debate in this field come at the end of each chapter and are included as aides-mémoire and to provide additional material for the reader to consider. Each chapter outlines an aspect of the basics of the method. The bullet point notes are intended to draw out the main points of the chapters for quick reference. There is, therefore, repetition of ideas in these.

QUICK REFERENCE NOTE

A Counselling Continuum

LEVEL 1	LEVEL 2	LEVEL 3	LEVEL 4
Interest in the person's concerns	Depression	Depression	Psychotic
	Broken relationships	Unhealed bereavements	Suicidal
	Bereavements	Long-standing anxieties	
	Decisions	Difficulties re study	
	Anxiety	'Don't know what's wrong"	
Homesickness	Work difficulties	Suicidal	
Wrong course	Homesickness		
Miserable	Wrong course		
Broken relationships	Miserable		
Work difficulties			
Bereavements			
Pastoral counselling (Listening skills)	**Counselling**	**Counselling/Psychotherapy**	**Psychiatric/medical/hospitalization**
Tutors	Counsellors	Counsellors only Accredited/ qualified	Medically qualified
Other students			
Administrative Staff			
Family/friends			
and also			
Nurses/Doctors ————	?. ?. ?.		
Student Advisers ————			
College Counsellors ————			
Accommodation Officers			
Careers Advisers			
This differs from counselling, which is time-consuming and would interfere with objectivity of academic process; danger of tutors getting too involved.	Formal contract to look at the issues.	Formal contract to look at the issues.	Referral out

AIMS OF THE BOOK

An introduction to brief psychodynamic psychotherapy

This book is intended as a basic introductory guide and as a quick reference handbook. Those seeking a more in-depth study might be interested in my first book, *Short Term Psychodynamic Psychotherapy: An Analysis of Key Principles*. This is a useful text to have alongside this guide and it will be referred to from time to time. I will abbreviate it to Rawson 2002 and the page references for simplicity. It was based on many years' research and goes into each area very thoroughly.

Concepts to be covered

Concepts to be covered in this guide include basic principles such as focus, contract, flexibility, activity, dynamics of the deadline, importance of the first session and endings.

Bullet point notes

The bullet point notes are ready to use as quick reference guides, aides-mémoire or handouts; they are copyrighted by *Fastpace*.

My hopes

I write from a position of faith in the approach. It is a treatment of choice, as you can see in the copy of the article in the quick reference notes at the end of Chapter One. I have not been compelled through pressure of numbers or financial limits to adopt this method. Rather, I have seen the good effects that can be achieved in a relatively short time. I want to see clients helped out of their pain and towards a more free existence in the shortest possible time. This is an approach that I have practised for some twenty-five years. Having been asked to teach the approach and to supervise those working in it for many years, I am often asked what it is. To answer this I have decided to provide a very basic guide to the practice of the method. This is in the hope that the approach may become more accessible to professionals and that more people may be helped more quickly by counsellors and therapists adopting the method.

I cannot claim that this method of therapy is my own. It is, in fact, rooted solidly in a tradition. Those who are interested in the history and development of brief psychodynamic psychotherapy might wish to refer to Rawson, 2002, pp. 39–47. Clearly I have adapted and modified the concept, as any therapist does. I learned the approach from the late Louis Marteau, and refined his eight model approach down to four to six sessions. This approach has been equally successful in colleges, in private practice, and in an employee assistance programme. My approach is not rigid or restrictive. It is flexible and the number of sessions offered is adapted to the particular needs of the client. Even so the mean tends to be four to six sessions.

By the end of the book it is hoped that therapists, supervisors, and trainers will feel clearer about its basics and more confident about practising as brief psychodynamic psychotherapists.

Limitations of this book

It is important to define the limits of what can be achieved in a basic guide such as this.

The book is short. Although of interest to a wide audience, it is aimed primarily at the experienced therapist and, therefore, all the basics involved in counselling and therapy are assumed. This makes it possible to focus just on those aspects of the therapeutic work that accelerate the process.

These ideas can make a difference

It is hoped that you will find that you can put the principles into practice very quickly. Many therapists who have grasped the basic ideas outlined in the first chapters have found their clients respond differently, even though they have not *consciously* done anything different.

Client and therapist comments

I have recorded below some comments made by therapists who were attending my courses in brief psychodynamic therapy and who consequently took on board the basics of brief therapy as outlined in this book. Some had been astonished at how their clients, whom they had been seeing for a long time, suddenly seem to shift forwards. For example:

'My client said it was such a relief to get to the point. I thought we were never going to get on with things.'

'Several of my clients seem to feel that they are ready to go now and that we've achieved what they wanted to.'

'I could not believe what we achieved in the last session.'

'I was aware that I had changed gear in my work with the client, I was much more focused.'

These statements were made after the first session of the course; that would be the equivalent of the first chapter here!

Confirming what you already know

In going through the book you may feel that you have not gained a whole new body of knowledge. You may feel that you knew it all anyway. That is all right. Now, however, perhaps you know that you know and will therefore continue your work in the brief method with more confidence. In fact, I expect that, for many of you, it will almost feel as if you now have been given permission to do what you've always done or wanted to do. In the knowledge that it is part of an approach that has a tradition, that has been around for years and that, indeed, began with Freud, you can feel more sure of what you are doing. For others some of the concepts may be quite new, and that is good too.

What the book is not

The book will, from time to time, highlight the differences between long- and short-term approaches or, indeed, highlight the similarities. It is not the intention of this work to debate whether one is better than the other. I am clearly expounding the benefits of the brief approach and attempting to give readers a certain knowledge and experience of the approach. It is then for the reader to make their own assessment as to its merits and whether it is a method that they wish to learn more about and to practise.

It would be very easy to become diverted from presenting the basics of brief therapy into an endless and unproductive debate as to which method is better, and my intention is to remain focused on the task in hand.

CHAPTER ONE

WHAT IS BRIEF PSYCHODYNAMIC PSYCHOTHERAPY? AN OVERVIEW

What is the approach? What do we understand by brief psychotherapy?

Well, first, what do we mean by short? By short I mean four to six sessions. However, this is flexible. If the client needs more then that will be what they will get. The aim is to complete the work in the shortest time possible so that the client is back on track again quickly. This therapy is not brief because of financial restraints nor because of pressure of numbers. Brief therapy is short because we hope to achieve what is required quickly. This is so that clients are able to get on with their lives without the burden that has brought them to therapy continuing to weigh them down. My research (Rawson, 2002), examining many studies, showed four to six sessions as the mean. This was with counsellors of all orientations and with clients and counsellors who had not intended to work in a brief way at all.

Colleges across the country also find that four sessions is average over the year. That means that some clients will be seen only once, while others might be seen as much as twenty times. Each contract will be made on an individual basis according to need. The contract is flexible.

To sum up, each client will be given what is needed.

Joint approach

The decision about how long will be made in conjunction with the client. One of the aspects of this approach is that it is a joint affair. This applies not just to the time scale but also to the focal issue. That is, to the main topic that is to be explored by the client. This joint approach encourages the client to work on their issues, to think about themselves and ultimately to become their own therapist. The therapist is simply facilitating their journey and being alongside them as they travel. The therapist will use all the skills at their disposal to help the client in their exploration. This includes helping the client to make connections with past and often buried issues. The baggage that remains, when problems have not been dealt with, can weigh heavily. Often, by working with the client on the past issue, they are enabled to move on more freely. One of the images I use with clients to explain this is that of a splinter.

Splinter image

If you have a splinter in your finger, you can mostly get on with things and ignore the splinter. But as you go along, if you press on the spot where the splinter is it hurts, and you cannot fully use that finger. Therapy helps to remove the emotional splinter. When we remove a real splinter we have to open up the wound and it bleeds and hurts, but then the splinter can be removed and we can immediately use the finger fully once again. It may take a little while to heal completely and sometimes a scar may remain, but essentially it is now all right. Similarly, it can be painful to explore emotional wounds. However, once they are brought out into the open and looked at they can be put into perspective. When they are accepted and 'emoted', then the burden can be put down and the client can be free to move on. By emoted, I mean that the emotions surrounding the issue and the emotional wound are allowed to 'be' and are acknowledged and expressed, perhaps with tears, or anger, or sadness. It is important to let the emotions out. Again, an image is useful here, this time that of a pressure cooker.

Pressure cooker image

The pressure cooker has a safety valve. It steams away. If the valve is blocked the pressure in the cooker can build up, and eventually there could be an explosion. Psychologically, the same thing can happen. If we hold on to or bury our feelings – anger or grief, for example – they can build up and keep slipping out in inappropriate circumstances. This can cause relationship difficulties in the home or at work. Sometimes emotions are buried for years and then something triggers them or there is such a build-up that, as in the pressure cooker image, the feelings can no longer be contained and there is some sort of crisis. This may take the form of an angry explosion, or perhaps a complete breakdown, where the person can no longer bear to carry on or no longer can bear their burden of responsibility. One may see a competent person suddenly totally unable to make decisions or carry out their job effectively. In others, the repressed emotions come out in the body through various illnesses. We see a definite correlation. for example. between ill health and the stress that befalls us at the time of a bereavement. If someone has too many stresses and too little support at the time of bereavement, ill health can ensue. McGannon (1996) gives some examples of the incidence of this. The scores that he refers to are in relation to the Holmes–Rahe scale that he also quotes (see quick reference notes at the end of the chapter). This scale is often quoted and is seen in both popular magazines and serious psychology books. It helps people to see how much change they are contending with in their lives, often as a result of a bereavement. It shows the devastating effect too much change all at once can have. We need, of course, to remember that some stress is good for us. Too little and we become bored, and that in itself is a stress, but this type of stress often spurs us to activity and out of our boredom. So to return to McGannon, he said:

> For those whose changes came too fast or too severe[ly], such as the group who scored more than 300, the chance of developing an illness in the near future (within a three month period) was about 80%, 51% in those who scored between 150 and 299, and 37% in those who scored less than 150. The severity of the illness corresponded to the score. Those diseases like heart diseases, ulcer disease, diabetes, alcoholism, cancers, depression, suicide, and certain infections, to less life-threatening annoyances, such as the common cold and indigestion. [McGannon, 1996, p. 188]

Being aware of the effect of stress, whether caused by a bereavement or some other change or loss, is only the beginning. One cannot rest there. It is the task of the individual, with or without the help of the therapist, to work out ways of alleviating the stress. Where this is not possible, it is necessary to build in better supports to help the person, as they slowly adapt to the new situation. The therapist can help by giving the support of a listening ear or by helping to unhitch past emotional baggage that has got caught up with the present situation. One might be unable to do anything to change the present trauma, but if one can release some of the weight of unfinished business from the past, the present situation might become more manageable. The therapist can sometimes enable the client to see their situation from a different perspective and so make the burden lighter. Simply allowing the client time and space, in a safe environment, to think over their situation and to make sense of what is going on, can also be helpful. In the process, if they are able to see new ways forward or new ways of approaching difficult situations, this too, can be good.

Psychodynamic

We call this approach, where the past issues are retrieved and explored, psychodynamic. Brief psychodynamic psychotherapy recognizes the effects of the unconscious and past events on the present situation. We do not just stay in the past. We are, as Louis Marteau (1986) says, 'reaching through the initial focus into the past 'to the very roots', but having dealt with the past we need to return to the present to go on, armed with what we have learned from the our past experiences. So we seek the emotional splinter – the focal issue.

Names of brief therapy.

There are many names for this brief approach, some twenty-five or so. These are listed in Rawson, 2002. One is 'Focal Therapy', a term coined by Balint, one of the key proponents of this method. One can understand why it is called this, since maintaining and keeping the focus in the approach is one of the factors that shortens the therapy. I shall return to this at a later point.

Who is brief psychodynamic therapy for?

This type of therapy is not for everyone. The same actually could be said of any therapy. I believe that we should aim to use the brief approach with everyone and only if it becomes apparent that it is not possible should we engage in longer therapy. This is entirely consistent with an earlier statement that I made that 'therapy should be as long as is necessary'.

Suitability of clients for brief therapy

There are certain conditions that need to be met for the brief therapy to be realistically possible. First, the clients need to be able to establish a reasonable rapport with the therapist. Sifneos, one of the early proponents of brief psychodynamic psychotherapy, would expect the clients to have at least one meaningful relationship in their life to date.

Second, the clients need to have a degree of insight and to be prepared to explore the possibility that the problem may have its roots in the past.

Third, they need to agree to the contract and to the area that the sessions are to focus on. As Sifneos states: 'Psychotherapy is always presented to the patient as a joint venture for the therapist and himself . . . If an area of conflict can be agreed upon, treatment will be undertaken' (Sifneos, 1968b, from Malan, 1971, p. 23).

Malan also quotes Balint as saying, 'The patient's and therapist's aim must be the same' (*ibid.*). This is such an important and obvious statement but is not always heeded. One recalls stories, apocryphal I hope, of clients who leave the college counsellor's office wondering why they have been so closely questioned about some issue in their past when, in fact, all they wanted to do was obtain a bus pass!

Can compulsory therapy work?

This need for agreement makes me wonder at times as to the wisdom and effectiveness of court orders that compel people to go for counselling before some desired outcome is permitted, e.g., the custody of a child. The British Association of Counselling and Psychotherapy's definition of counselling refers to it being a 'freely entered into activity'. College senior staff, not infrequently, refer students as part of a disciplinary procedure; again the compulsion element militates against successful action. Can counsellors take on such a client? I would suggest that, if in the first session it is clear that the client is ONLY there through compulsion, it would be questionable to continue. If that is but one of their reasons, and they can be helped to see the intrinsic value of the sessions and, having become aware of this, choose to stay, that is another matter.

Circumscribed focal issue

There needs also to be an identifiable issue that the client wishes to explore. A 'circumscribed' focal issue, as Sifneos would express it. This means that the client and therapist can identify a specific emotional area about which the client is concerned, and on which they wish to work. Very often the client will come for therapy in some kind of emotional crisis triggered by a present event or situation. While it can be helpful to see the client in the throes of such a crisis, this type of therapy is not a therapy that deals only with crises. It aims to get to the very roots of a problem and thus help the client deal with the deeper issues, often stemming from the past. Otherwise these keep rearing their heads in the present to cause problems.

Patterns of adaptive behaviour

In dealing with past issues the matter does not rest there. The client needs to be helped to deal with the patterns of adaptive behaviour that they may have got into. This may take a while, but does not necessarily mean that they need to be in therapy while they do it. Once they understand some of the ways in which they can break a habit, they can go on their way and be their own therapist. This is one of the features of the brief approach.

Motivation (Rawson, 2002, p. 159)

If the client is not motivated to explore their issues, to understand the problem, and to attempt to change, little will happen. This is linked with the point about choice and freely choosing counselling therapy that was made earlier.

Therapy is not an easy option. To explore issues that are sufficiently painful to have been covered up, avoided, or maladapted to is not easy. It can be painful and difficult. Clients leave the therapist's office, at times, describing how they feel as follows:

'I feel like a wet rag.'
'I feel totally drained.'
'I feel exhausted.'

Later, however, this can give way to other statements, such as

'I felt lighter.'
'I felt as if I were waking up after a deep sleep.'
'I look back at what I talked about earlier and it was as if all of that belonged to someone else.'

Clients who are not suitable

Clients who are not suitable obviously include those who do not meet the conditions mentioned above. These are people who are unable to show any insight about themselves and who cannot see the relevance or understand the process of therapy, or those who are unable to find any kind of focus. There are clients who are unable to accept the conditions for brief therapy, who are not willing to work on issues, or are unable to establish a rapport with the therapist. To this I would add someone who is out of touch with reality, someone, for example, seeing little green men who are telling them what to do or say. Such a person needs to see a psychiatrist and to be on the appropriate medication before they attempt therapy. Someone under the influence of drugs or drink would also be an unsuitable candidate for brief therapy, or any talking therapy. If someone is in the throes of a crisis, e.g., a road accident, exams, a death, this may not be the time for brief therapy, although it might well be the time for some kind of supportive therapy. The client in these circumstances needs to be given options, with client and therapist jointly deciding what to do. For example, one client might decide that they do wish to continue the therapeutic work that had been planned, despite being in the middle of some kind of other crisis. For another client it might be appropriate to postpone sessions altogether, for yet another it might be best to alter the contract to talk of the current crisis situation and later on resume the original contract. For yet another, the present crisis might have brought a former trauma to the surface and this could be the trigger point for some useful exploration of the past that, in its turn, helps the present situation.

One needs to stress flexibility and negotiation in these situations and these are features of the brief approach.

Angela Molnos has listed counterindications for therapy (see sheet in the quick reference notes at the end of this chapter, entitled: 'Selection of patients: dynamic brief psychotherapy notes'). She has written about brief psychodynamic psychotherapy (Molnos, 1995) and for a while worked at the Dympna Centre, where I trained, and worked alongside Louis Marteau.

Malan's review of his own research team and that of other experts in the field observes that: 'It is important to note the conspicuous absence of severe psychopathology as a contraindication. This also accords with our own evidence' (Malan, 1971, p. 23). This is another way of saying that brief therapy is for a much wider group of patients than some would believe. As Wolberg, one of the key early proponents of the method, says: 'The best strategy, in my opinion, is to assume that every patient, irrespective of diagnosis, will respond to short term treatment unless he proves himself to be refractory to it' (Wolberg, 1965, p. 140).

How is brief therapy done?

How do we make therapy brief? In beginning to examine this, it may be helpful to think about the analogy of a sprint versus a long-distance race. A sprinter has a certain pent up energy that is used in the burst of activity required in this type of race, which lasts but a short time. This is quite different from the long-distance run that requires a different sort of energy. An energy that has to be more sustained, conserved, and measured out so that the long-distance runner reaches the goal. In brief therapy we are sprinting. This applies to both therapist and client. I will return to this analogy later. Let us explore how one does this brief therapy.

Focus

One needs to be very focused. There is not time to explore every avenue, so one needs to target the key issues and work hard around these or those closely linked with them.

Activity

Brief therapy involves a certain activity on the part of the therapist, who has to draw the client back if they wander off the subject, or question how this seemingly unrelated area fits in with the agreed focus.

Therapeutic alliance

It is important for the client and therapist to have an agreed focus and time frame. This will be reached after a period of exploration. This process already involves the client in the therapeutic relationship and creates the therapeutic alliance. In searching with the therapist for the focus and in explaining why they are there, the client's motivation becomes apparent. If they are not motivated it will be very hard to come to this agreement.

Flexibility

The therapist needs to be very flexible in working briefly, being ready to adapt skills to fit the client and to renegotiate both contract and time scale if this seems necessary. I believe that if the therapist has experience this helps to speed the therapy. This is because the experienced therapist is less afraid to experiment. The person with experience has a range of skills to call upon and has seen many problems over the years, all of which contribute to the body of knowledge now available to the therapist. Flexibility of skills means that the therapist will use whatever tool seems appropriate at the time. This approach allows for a 'fusion' of skills and experience. I like this word, one that Wolberg uses in his writings about short-term therapy in the 1960s. So, as you see, this approach is not a new one at all! Nowadays, the word used would probably be 'integrative', the term 'eclectic' having seen better days. The concept of fusion seems to me to imply a seamlessness in the use of many skills and that is how I believe it should be.

Who can do it?

Because we are, so to speak, sprinting in this method of therapy, there is a certain energy required of the therapist and an alertness, and attention to detail. I believe that the approach is best handled by an experienced therapist. This is simply because the experienced therapist will perhaps be less thrown by anything that the client brings up, will have more skills at their disposal, and more confidence to adapt and try new things than the newly qualified counsellor. There is, however, debate about this issue, since often the experienced counsellor may have a certain prejudice against the brief approach and will therefore block progress by virtue of this. The new therapist, who has come freshly to the approach and who is prepared to believe in it, can in fact achieve very good results despite inexperience. So there are pros and cons here!

Involvement

I have already alluded to the sprinting idea and to the flexibility of skills that make the approach an active one. The therapist is active and so is the client. The client is expected to be involved and indeed involvement is seen to be a very important principle in the approach. In fact, based on my own research into this method, my 'conjecture is that client involvement is central to the shortening process' (Rawson, 2002, p. 276).

Ability to handle stress

There is another aspect to be considered by those thinking of working in the brief method. The therapist working in this way needs to be able to sustain a large amount of stress. There is a quick turnover of clients if you are seeing people for just a short time. Therefore, one sees a high number of different traumatic situations in people's lives in the course of a year. A full-time counsellor, who is abiding by the guidelines of, for example, the university therapist, and who sees, say, four people per day or sixteen per week for a number of sessions each, may well see between eighty and 150 different clients a year. I have found that as I have become more experienced I can see less clients per day if I am to do each one justice. I think that four is sufficient for one day. I have found that other experienced colleagues who were also working in the brief approach agree with this. Earlier in my career I used to see more but I now realize the folly of this. Is it that one builds up a certain residue of pain in one's encounters with clients and there are limits to this, despite the 'detached involvement' we endeavour to acquire in our training and the protection afforded by supervision and therapy? One of the tasks of supervision is to help therapists to separate their own issues from the clients. It also provides a place where the therapist can debrief after a heavy session with a client and offload if necessary.

Therapy is a compulsory part of training for most therapists and contributes to the therapist being able to remain unentangled from their clients' material. Ongoing supervision is a professional requirement for the accredited therapist (see British Association of Counsellors and Psychotherapists' (BACP) regulations).

Because there is a frequent turnover of clients the therapist needs to be able to handle loss well. This will be covered later on.

One has to be ready to change gear very quickly, not just within each session but also between each client. All the clients will be at different stages of their process and each brings a very different issue. I suggest that, because the turnover is greater than with longer term clients, this is a more wearing experience than may be the case for longer term work.

Therapists' comments

Having stressed the more difficult aspects of this, I want also to emphasize that there is great satisfaction in seeing clients move on positively after such a brief time. This is very rewarding and stimulating.

Therapists attending courses to learn about the brief approach describe their feelings about the experience using words such as: 'exciting', 'thought provoking', 'challenging', 'interesting', 'energizing'. Others observe that it is: 'tiring', 'active', 'focused', 'freeing', 'incisive', 'stimulating', 'intriguing'.

A great privilege and joy

Practitioners who are alongside clients who come into the counselling suffering and who leave after just a few sessions clearly more able to cope and happier, describe the experience as 'a great privilege and joy'.

Therapist optimism

The therapist sets the scene for optimism and for the effectiveness of the approach. It is good to point out that belief in the approach is one of the criteria for enabling it to happen. The therapist's attitude will affect how the process is talked about and worked with. This will influence the client and the outcome. The reader wanting to practise in this way, needs to take this on board so as not to sabotage the possibility of the work being brief.

Belief in the method

Since one of the facets of this approach is to inspire hope that the work can be achieved in a short time, it must be realized that it will not be so if, deep down, the therapist does not really believe it.

How can one learn to believe in it? By talking to those who have worked in this way, but with an open mind. By reading about the method and the results that can be achieved, as you are doing here. By trying it for yourself, but with an open mind. By attending a training course in the method for yourself. By talking to clients who have worked in this way successfully. By undergoing a brief contract of therapy for yourself. By realizing that therapy to overcome an issue or problem is quite different from a training therapy or from therapy to understand the maximum possible about yourself.

Summary of basic principles

At this point it is relevant to highlight some of the key principles to which we have already drawn attention. I take for granted the motivation of the client. Then we referred to the short number of sessions, the active and focused approach, the joint enterprise of client and therapist, the flexibility of the therapist, and the enabling of the client to become their own therapist. In relation to the latter point, one of the ways that we do this is by teaching. We explain to the client what we are doing and why, and help them actively to explore their own issues.

Detective image

I often use the image of a detective in trying to explain the process of therapy to a client. In a way, both client and therapist are detectives, examining the evidence rigorously. Just as a detective or forensic scientist might be examining minute pieces of evidence under a microscope, in our focusing on one area, the key issue, we are doing likewise. We piece together bits and pieces of facts, memories, and feelings and attempt to help the client to make sense of it. This is not just an academic or theoretical exercise. We help them to *re-experience f*eelings and emotions as necessary and to learn new patterns or ways of reacting. In this we are also taking on a teaching role.

17

Incisive and sensitive

Two other principles are very important: incisiveness and sensitivity. We will be returning to these and other aspects, such as the importance of the first session, and the therapeutic alliance or agreement as to what is to be worked upon. I have not, as yet, stressed the *early establishment* of this alliance. It is important that this agreement is reached very soon in the process, so that the work begins straight away. To achieve this the therapist will, at times, be quite incisive and probing, especially as the initial focus is being established. Sensitivity, however, is an overriding principle, so this incisiveness and, indeed, the quickness must not appear to be intrusive or superficial. Rather, this is experienced as holding and reassuring, as the client feels that the therapist is fully on their wavelength and really understands their pain. The therapist, in this way, inspires hope that something can be done about it and that they, the clients, are in control.

Following the quick reference notes below we return to the various aspects mentioned in the overview above to examine them in more detail, beginning with the focus.

The reader is reminded that the bullet point notes that follow are intended to draw out the main points of the chapter for quick reference and possibly for use as handouts or aides-mémoire. There is, therefore, repetition of ideas in these.

QUICK REFERENCE NOTES

Focal and short-term psychodynamic psychotherapy

- Focal psychotherapy is especially useful in short-term psychotherapy.
- Average 4–6 sessions, but can be as few as one session and as many as are needed.
- Focal and short-term psychotherapy is an approach where client and therapist work together on an agreed focal area within a specific time scale.
- It is an approach that allows for a wide range of therapy methods to be used.
- It utilizes the clients' capacity to think about themselves and ultimately to become their own therapists.
- Since client and therapist are working on a clear focus, this facilitates evaluation of the work achieved.
- It is psychodynamic since it recognizes the effects of the unconscious and past events in the present situation for the client.
- It is best used in the hands of an experienced therapist who is able to adopt a flexible approach.
- It is an active approach.

Suitability of client

- Has to be able to find a focus – at least a general one.
- Has to show indications of insight.
- Has to agree to the terms on offer.
- The client's need – not the therapist's.
- Has to wish to work on the issues in order to change or move on.
- Has to be able to establish a rapport with the therapist.

Counter-indications to suitability of client for short-term psychotherapy

- Out of touch with reality.
- Inability to understand the process of therapy; i.e., unable to agree a contract to work on issues.
- Resistence (undue and persistent) to any concept of the influence of the past events on the present.
- Under the influence of drugs or drink.
- Under pressure to attend for therapy by external authorities.
- In the throes of a crisis, e.g., a death, an exam (supportive therapy more likely to be required at this time but client and therapist need to discuss options).

Selection of patients – dynamic brief psychotherapy (Molnos, 1987, personal communication)

1. EXCLUSION CRITERIA
Who is not suitable for DBP with [its] strong initial confrontation of defences.

Principal diagnostic exclusion criterion:
Thought processes get disturbed under confrontation of resistance

Psychological exclusion criterion:
Weak ego

Psychiatric exclusion criteria:
Previous psychotic decompensation
Paranoid conditions
Poor impulse control

Pathologies and factual exclusion criteria:
Very long-term psychiatric in-patient treatment
Repeat ECT-treatment
Destructive acting out against others, i.e. physical violence
Serious suicide attempt (especially manic depressive or schizophrenic)
Other gross self-destructive acting out (e.g.anorexia, bulimia, etc.)

2. SELECTION CRITERIA:WHO IS ESPECIALLY SUITABLE FOR BDP?
Psychological selection criteria:
Motivation for change (as distinct from wanting only symptom relief)

Ability to relate to the therapist
Ego – strength to withstand confrontation
Capacity for insight.
Pathologies:
Neuroses with oedipal focus
Neuroses with focus on loss
Obsessional and phobic neuroses with more than one focus
Long standing pscyhoneurotic disorders and characterological problems with no clear focus.

3. FURTHER REMARKS ON SELECTION
In principle, the earlier the damage the more the defences are likely to have grown and to be part of the psychic structure. If this is the case and the defences are challenged by the therapist, the patient will feel attacked in his inner core. As a result he might drop out and /or his thought processes might get disturbed. On the other hand, strong initial confrontation, leading to a successful breakthrough, is possible even in cases of early damage provided the patient has ego strength.

4.LITERATURE
H. Davanloo ed. 1980 pp. 75–189
D. H. Malan 1979 pp. 209–253
P. E. Sifneos 1979 pp. 22–39
L. R. Wolberg 1980 pp, 30–34.

Motivation

Quotation from *Frontier of Brief Psychotherapy*, with regard to assessing the client's motivation

> 'We have emphasized the importance not merely of motivation for *treatment*, but motivation for *insight*; in Sifneos' statement, 'There should be motivation for *change*, not motivation for *symptom relief*' (1968b), the words are different but the meaning is essentially the same.
>
> The criteria relevant to motivation to which Sifneos directs his attention are as follows (these are taken from Sifneos, 1968a: see also Sifneos, 1972, pp. 85ff):
>
> 1.   An ability to recognize that the symptoms are psychological in nature.
> 2.   A tendency to be introspective and to give an honest and truthful account of emotional difficulties.
> 3.   Willingness to participate actively in the treatment situation.
> 4.   Curiosity and willingness to understand oneself.
> 5.   Willingness to change, explore, experiment.
> 6.   Realistic expectations of the results of psychotherapy.
> 7.   Willingness to make reasonable sacrifices in terms of time and fees.
>
> To these criteria, McGuire(1968) has added two that are probably implied by Sifneos, namely:
>
> 8.   That the patient should not demand that particular symptoms should be relieved.
> 9.   That he should not regard the problem as being purely concerned with the present situation or as being purely external. [Malan, 1976, pp. 22–23]

Basic principles of focal and short-term psychotherapy

(It is a pre-requisite that the client is MOTIVATED!)

- Active
- Focused
- Importance of first session
- Early establishment of the therapeutic alliance
- Joint venture
- Therapist attitude
- Time limited
- Flexible therapist
- Psychodynamic
- Teaching
- Enabling client to become own therapist
- Incisiveness
- Sensitivity

Holmes–Rahe scale

Table 1 The scale of stressors for major life events

Event	Points
Death of a spouse	100
Divorce	73
Marital separation	65
Death of close family member	63
Change in health of a family member	44
Death of a close friend	37

Source: McGannon (1996), based on Holmes & Rahe (1967).

Table 2 The scale of stressors for changes in way of life

Nature of change	Points
Being fired from job	45
Retirement	45
Type of work	36
Living conditions	25
Recreation activities	19
Social activities	19
Sleeping habits	19
Number of family meetings	15
Eating habits	15

Source: See Table 1.

'Focal and short-term psychotherapy is a treatment of choice' (Rawson, 1992, *Counselling*)

I read, with interest, Stephen Palmer's interview of Professor Windy Dryden with reference to brief short-term psychotherapy (February 1992). Professor Dryden quotes John Rowan as saying, 'We are short-changing individuals who come for counselling if we don't encourage them to see that counselling is an opportunity for them to reflect on themselves in the context of their entire life. We can't do that,' says John, 'if we are only offering brief psychotherapy.'

I would like to ask who's short changing whom?

I believe the principles of brief and focal psychotherapy make it clear that we are not short-changing clients by offering them this type of counselling/therapy. Brief and focal therapy is a *treatment of choice* – not simply a method to use because financial or resource restraints so dictate, as Professor Dryden implies.

I have been spurred to write this article in the hope that many potential clients may benefit as more counsellors become aware of the value of the focal and brief approach.

In my experience a large number of individuals approach counselling/therapy with the assumption, encouraged by popular opinion and their therapist that their problem will take a very long time to resolve. This may be the case if, for example, their presenting 'depression' has been with them for several years. Some will have been receiving medication for many years, and will anyway be sceptical as to whether a counsellor can help. It is my contention and experience that very many people can be helped significantly in less than ten sessions, many in as few as 2–6 sessions. By significantly, I mean reach a point

(1)   where they understand the roots of their depression, often from a traumatic experience in childhood;
(2)   where they have discharged the emotions relating to that; and
(3)   where they are in a position to say, 'I feel I can cope with my life now – I'll know how to deal with similar events if they occur.'

I believe the majority of people approach counselling therapy because they are 'unhappy' – there is usually something they wish to change and they hope to feel better. Many more people would approach counselling/therapy if they had confidence that they could be helped in a few (2–10) sessions. These they could afford – whereas the idea of ongoing therapy for six months or years may prevent them even considering therapy. Many more could be helped in this way if they were aware of the focal and short-term method.

The focal and short-term method

So, what is it? It is not simply a limited contract in terms of sessions, although the limited time helps, of course.

Who does not know the effect of a deadline? Having a limited time is a powerful way of concentrating the mind and effort. Focal and brief therapy is more than this. It is also about the focus of the sessions. The presenting problem is the starting point. In focal therapy the client and therapist need to agree the focus of the sessions. Sifneos (1968) says: 'Psychotherapy is always presented to the patient as a joint venture. If an area can be agreed upon, treatment will be undertaken.' The client also needs to be able to grasp the idea that the problem may well have its roots in the past. As client and therapist explore the presenting issue in the search for the focal area and the contract – the work has already begun. A simple question like, 'When do you first recall being depressed?', can lead directly through the presenting problem of depression to the traumatic episode of the child. It is likely that this area of the person's life will become the focal area to be explored and the counselling work will focus around the repercussions of this for the client.

The therapist's expectation that change can occur in a relatively short time no doubt serves as a motivator and has a certain power of suggestion. It can also inspire hope. Perhaps the rapid results I see have something to do with my own confident expectation that change can occur in a very limited time if the client is prepared to work on themselves.

Resistance

Resistance is tackled as it arises; clients being helped gently to voice fears about change and being challenged to continue working on the agreed contract – or not – it is, of course, their choice! Here again the limited number of sessions agreed helps. The fact that the whole painful process may be completed in maybe eight sessions makes it possible for the client to stay with the process.

Counselling is painful. Clients talk of it being 'draining', 'exhausting', 'feeling like a wet rag', and so to know it has a definite end is reassuring and enabling.

The focal and brief approach can be a particularly intense and demanding form of therapy for both client and therapist. The particular approach I use is a psychodynamic one using the newer therapies. I am inclined to the view expressed by Wolberg (1965) that 'the focal and short-term approach required a sophistication born of the wisdom of experience'. There is not the time to make mistakes – to miss cues. Also the greater the experience of the therapist the more flexible she/he is likely to be, with more psychotherapeutic 'tools' at his/her disposal. Flexibility on the part of the therapist is important. Awareness of dependency, transference issues, resistance, body language, the use of silence, fantasy, etc., are important.

Activity

Activity is essential in focal and brief therapy – again to quote Wolberg (1965), 'Anathema to short-term therapy is passivity in the therapist'.

Activity is also asked of the clients. They are encouraged to become their own therapist and to work on themselves between sessions – to do 'homework'.

As one client wrote after she'd completed her therapy in eleven sessions:

> If I were to visualise the whole experience, I'd say it was as if I was trying to paint my life but the only colours I had were black and white. Counselling gave me the primary colours to add depth and texture but most importantly I held the brush.

The method of Focal and Brief Psychotherapy is not new – Freud's treatment of Gustav Mahler was achieved in a few hours and his analysis of Sandor Ferenczi was also limited to a number of weeks. Alexander and French were exponents in the 1940s, Malan, Sifneos, Wolberg, and Balint in the 1960s and 1970s, and Davanloo more latterly. I am, myself, indebted to Louis Marteau, Director of the Dympna Centre (London) who taught me existential short-term therapy in the 1970s. That is a flexible, active, time limited psychodynamically based integrative approach. An overriding view that stays with me from the years I spent training, both in the long- and short-term methodology, is the most persuasive aspect of cost-effectiveness – that is the alleviation of people's 'pain' in the shortest time possible. In the process of the therapy, they will acquire skills that will remain with them. They do not need a therapist to ensure ongoing development. I find in my twenty years of practicing [*sic*] this method that the number of sessions to achieve real change and free a particular block has reduced and may now be as few as one!

A median number is four, with 10–12 being the usual maximum. The number of sessions offered will vary from client to client and is negotiated.

The context

I believe the context in which the therapy is undertaken may influence the number of sessions. For example, working within a GP practice or an education institution may facilitate rapid progress. These contexts have already implicitly contributed to the establishment of trust, confidentiality and credibility. In private practice it may be necessary to spend more time, perhaps two or three sessions, ensuring these essential features of the relationship are established. This would take the median number of sessions to six or seven, and would seem consistent with the findings (referred to by Rogawski, 1981) of Butcher and Koss (1978 and Garfield (1978). They found that a large percentage of clients termination after 6–8 sessions. This, it should be noted, related also to clients of therapists who did not claim to advocate the short-term approach.

Dr Dryden hopes that educational and training establishments will begin to inform students about this approach and I wholeheartedly endorse this, although I think there are more issues to be addressed as to whether the training should be geared to the experienced or to beginners. Can a beginner be as effective in this method as someone with more experience? A trainee counsellor will not have the experience or knowledge of a variety of therapeutic approaches to bring to the therapy and so might be less effective. However, neither will they have developed therapist resistance to the brief approach and so might prove more effective in this method than someone trained in longer-term methods first.

There are already training programmes in specific approaches to brief therapy in existence in this country.

CHAPTER TWO

FOCUS

The importance of having a focus has been pointed to earlier. How then do we arrive at this focus and, having found it, how do we keep to it?

Finding the focus

The therapist can ask many questions that can help the client to find the focus. Important ones include the following:

- What made you come to see a therapist at this time?
- When did the feeling/ problem start?
- Have you felt this way before?
- Can you give me an example?
- Can you tell me about it?

The therapist invites the client to say what it is that has brought them to therapy and what it is that made them do so at this point in time. These are very important questions that begin to help the client to focus on their problem. A general statement such as: '*I am depressed*' would need to be unwrapped somewhat. One could ask what that means. Is the person sad? Are they suicidal? What does the depression make them feel like doing?

Beware of making assumptions

One needs to be careful not to make assumptions. As we've already observed, the word 'depressed' can mean very different things to different people. For one person, it can indeed mean that they are thinking of killing themselves, for another it is simply that they are feeling a bit down or fed up. To understand what it means to the individual we need examples and detail.

Be specific

Both client and therapist need to have a clear idea as to what they are working on – a clear focus – for the therapy to work well, so asking for specifics and examples helps to do this. Sometimes it may take more than one session to really get to the focus but the search for it is imperative. Only when we know what we are working on can we in some sense assess a successful outcome. Sometimes there is an initial focus and as we begin to explore this with the client a more strategic one emerges. This 'strategic focus' then is what we focus on. Sifneos talks of 'circumscribing the focus' as one of the shortening factors. I refer to the 'strategic focus'. Balint named his method of therapy 'focal therapy'. All of us are highlighting the importance of knowing what it is and of working with it.

In searching for the focus one 'goes for the jugular', 'pins the patient to the floor', 'gets to the point'. These phrases are used in talking of finding the focus. I have sometimes been challenged about what seems like violent language. One is merely stressing the importance of keeping to the central point and not waffling around. In fact, the client is usually relieved that the therapy is getting to the point. It gives them hope and confidence that the therapist has understood where their issue or problem lies. They themselves may be more clear as to the problem because the therapist's questions may have enabled them to be less confused. If we went to the doctor with a bad hip and he started to ask about our hand or arm we would feel rather impatient and wonder why he was wandering off the point of our visit. In the psychological sphere, I suggest, it is the same. There may be interconnections between the different pains in our bodies as there can be interconnections in the emotional and psychological spheres as well. However, the client needs to feel that we have listened to their original problem. From there we may move to related areas when necessary.

Questions to help the client focus

Questions that we might use to focus down on the client's issue might be as follows:

- When did you first experience this problem?
- How old were you at the time?
- Can you give me an example?
- Can you be more specific?

How does this feel to the client?

On my courses I ask trainees how they have felt as 'client' when I used such questions with them. The students make comments such as the following:

'I felt pinned down . . . but that was good.'

'I felt backed into a corner . . . I guess I'd have had to deal with what I came for.'

'I wasn't going to be let off the hook.'

'I felt you really wanted to understand exactly what I was saying.'

'I felt relief. Someone was really going to help me sort what was going on.'

'I felt really uncomfortable but safe all at once. I found myself saying things I didn't know I knew.'

'It made me feel hopeful.'

Interestingly, the observing members of the training group often perceive the process as almost brutal and are at times cringing for the one working with me. They are then surprised at the positive comments that come back from the 'client'. That is, that they have felt *held, listened to, understood, kept to the point, homed in on, not allowed to deviate from the task in hand.*

I have found, too, that when a training group practises the art of trying to focus, some will have had the experience of losing focus and being allowed to wander off the point. They discover that as 'client' they feel disappointed and let down at the deviation and prefer the more actively focusing approach. This is so, even though at times they felt almost pinned down and uncomfortable, because it also gave them a sense that they were getting to where they needed to.

Louis Marteau used to use the analogy of nailing one foot to the floor; he meant by this that once the focus was set the client could move all around it, but just so far. He, too, was challenged about the use of a brutal kind of image. It is simply a graphic analogy to make a point.

I wonder if the client feels 'held', an expression that is so often used in therapy, in the same way that babies would seem to prefer, a firm hold rather than a wishy-washy one. It perhaps makes them feel more safe. Is this what we really mean by it in this therapy context? This has prompted me to go to the dictionary for definitions. It is hard to see which of the meanings, which cover a whole column, can be applied to the way that we tend to use this word in therapy. If this were a live course it would be opportune to spend a few moments wondering with the group. However, mindful of the 'one foot to the floor' we need to very soon relate the discussion or, in this context, the diversion, back to the point, i.e., finding the focus and how the questions that 'zoom in' can give the client the feeling of being 'held'.

Naming the focus sets the scene

Once one has found the focus we have a kind of heading for our work. Thereafter, the thoughts or memories that surface seem to relate even though, initially, the relationship may not be very clear. For example, once I was teaching a class of children religious education (RE) and for this particular lesson I played a piece of classical music and asked them to write a poem. All thirty pupils wrote the most lovely prayers, assuming that that was expected because it was, after all, an RE lesson. I then went on to an English class; I played the same music and asked them also to write a poem inspired by the music. None of these was religious in any way at all but referred to a range of subjects. It would seem that the title of the lesson gave the backcloth and therefore inspired appropriately. I suggest that once we have named our focal area everything else then relevant to that tends to emerge.

Some techniques are particularly useful in helping the client to find the focus, e.g., a body memory exercise. This will be explained in greater detail in a later chapter.

Triggers for emotional problems

Anniversaries

Anniversaries may be the trigger for a problem. The anniversary of a death, or losing a job, or the breaking up of a relationship may be the trigger. The body somehow remembers these traumatic events even though, consciously, we have moved on and forgotten all about them. It sometimes only emerges as we explore the situation, because the client has come to us complaining of depression and one asks: 'Is this time of year or this date of any significance?' Often, it then transpires that there was a death, or a break-up of the family, a redundancy, or an accident exactly at this time, but years ago. Sometimes the memory is immediately accompanied by tears or anger. There is often a sense of recognition by the client as they see that this is what is the cause of their present depression.

World events

World events can trigger problems for our clients, perhaps a memory or an actual event in the here and now. For example, someone whose father or husband or daughter is off to war. Or where another member of the family has been killed or injured, or is fighting overseas and is in danger. The therapist needs to be aware of what is going on, as far as possible, and alert enough to at least question in this area if it seems appropriate. Even television soaps can lead to a number of clients coming to the therapist with similar problems that have been opened up by what they have seen.

Jean

A situation arose with Jean that exemplifies this. The therapy had been progressing nicely around her issues and then one day she came into the session and seemed to have gone backwards a long way.

Jean said, 'I felt as if I had been making progress and in fact had been feeling really good since last week, but then yesterday I suddenly seemed to be so miserable and depressed and I still am.'

I asked, 'Can you recall when you were last OK?'

Jean: 'Yes, until about 4 o'clock when I collected the children from school. It was after that.'

I asked her to retrace every step of what happened after that. Something must have happened. You may recall the detective idea referred to earlier. If we can examine the time period with a magnifying glass we may well make sense of this change of mood. So Jean thought back through what she had been doing. I pointed out to her that sometimes it can be something as little as a small paragraph in a newspaper that can remind us of something and send us plummeting down to the depths. So I requested that she be very specific about what she had done, who she had been with and what they had been talking about. She mentioned a TV soap that she had

watched. As it happened I had watched the same programme; there had been an episode of a miscarriage in it.
Although this was not the subject that had been the focus
of our sessions, she had mentioned a miscarriage incidentally when talking about the number of children that she
had. Jean mentioned the programme and went on to the
next thing that she had been doing. Because I had seen
the programme I had a hunch that the miscarriage scene
was the cause of her lowered mood. I stopped her story
and asked her to go back to the programme.

Penny: 'Can you remember what it was about?' Jean
skirted over the story, so I asked, 'Were you feeling all
right before it?'

Jean: 'Yes'.

Penny: 'So was there anything in the programme that
upset you?'

Jean then recalled the miscarriage scene and began
to be a little tearful. As we talked about her own miscarriage it became clear that this programme had indeed been
the trigger for her sudden gloom. While the sadness was
real and present it did not mean that the other work
we had been doing together had gone back to square
one. This had been her fear and had added to her concern.
Attaching the feeling of sadness to where it belonged
enabled her to move on once more with her other
concerns.

In this instance, I was in a lucky position in that I had
happened to see the programme and was able to put two
and two together and so questioned her carefully about
the programme. Jean was also fortunate because she had
been conscious of feeling quite good and then had very
recently noticed the change. I always stress with the client
that if they find themselves, as Jean did, with a sudden

change in mood that seems inexplicable, it is really worth examining very, very carefully every single thing that has happened between the time of being all right and not being all right. Our minds react quickly and the mood change follows on quickly, too. It might be a passing thought, a word, a memory, something done or not done by someone else, something we've read or heard, a tune, a bird song, or a place. Anything can trigger thought and therefore our moods. If we are to become our own therapists on such occasions, we need to look very carefully at our situation. Teaching the client to become their own therapist is, you will recall, one of the aims of brief therapy.

Changes

Changes in the context that the person is living in can be the cause of the problem. Sometimes there are just too many negatives all at once and they weigh the client down.

The Heimler social functioning concept

The Heimler social functioning concept indicates a balance of stresses with which we can cope and one where it becomes unsustainable and the person finds it very difficult to cope. There is a three-year course that one can take in this approach and one then can register to be a practitioner of the concept. However, there is still merit in touching on the ideas held here. Essentially we look with the client at the key areas in life.

The questions are divided into two sections, the first of which deals with:

(i)   work and hobbies, since these are often the areas that people find easiest to talk about;

(ii)   finance and whether the clients can save;

(iii) primary family;

(iv) secondary family;

(v)   how they feel about themselves.

The second section is very revealing, in particular with respect to a question that is looking for any indication of suicidal thoughts. The very fact that the question is asked gives the client permission to reveal their feelings in this regard very quickly. These questions cover :

(i)   whether alcohol or drugs are a problem;

(ii)   whether the person ever wishes they were dead;

(iii) some general question as to how they feel about life in general.

Of the first five areas a person can usually handle as many as three of these being bad, but at four they are becoming rather wobbly and with five even worse. However, we can help them to strengthen each of the areas. We can ask if they would like to explore these various areas with us so that we can enable them to build up sufficient positives to be able to dare to look at the real problem areas. For example, if work is hated, we can encourage greater focus on hobbies, if finance is in trouble, we can encourage them perhaps towards a part-time job, or in exploring how they spend their money, which may allow us to encourage less eating out and more home cooking, for instance. We can ask how much is spent on cigarettes and drink. Or whether the private schooling for their children is really necessary, or the holiday abroad.

Be aware of the ordinary

It is relevant to be aware of the ordinary things such as whether the client sleeping and eating. Students, for example, especially around the times of exams, sometimes tend to forget this. If they study through the nights and do not sleep or eat they can end up hallucinating and being utterly stressed out, scarcely able to think straight. Before calling in the psychiatrist it is often a good thing to check when they last ate or slept.

Picking up the emotion

In the encounter with the client, the therapist needs to be aware all the time of 'the music' beneath the words. At times, the client's outer exterior does not reflect what is being expressed in words. The words do not tally with the body language, the tone of voice, or the expression on the face. Sometimes the patient may be smiling or seeming quite chirpy, but they are in fact expressing something really sad. It is often to cover up the depth of real feeling. This needs to be explored with the client.

At times, this contradiction needs to become the focus of the session, rather than the agreed focus. I have formerly stressed the need for an agreed focus and this is not a contradiction. The emotion that one detects is in the here and now in the counselling room and so, if we check that our peception is right, it is true and real. We need to see what it is about; it may connect with the original agreed focus and may take us more deeply into that. It may also reveal a more important issue that needs to be addressed and then the focus needs to be renegotiated. There is no point in looking at a theoretical or academic issue, even if previously agreed, if the emotion is clearly elsewhere.

Projective identification: an aspect of countertransference

Sometimes the therapist picks up the emotion of the client in their own body, or in the feeling present in the room.

Client's body language

When the client has decided to trust the therapist and is willing to open up and reveal the real reason for their visit, very often their body will turn towards the therapist.

Under the microscope

Once we have a focus, we put it under the microscope so that it is examined in great detail. It will contain elements of other conflicts and patterns. Having this focus concentrates the mind of the therapist and client, as does having a time limit.

In the first session

This process of finding the focus and beginning the 'work' of therapy takes place in the first session. The first session is very important in the brief approach and merits a chapter of its own (Chapter Three).

QUICK REFERENCE NOTES

Finding the focus

General exploratory questions

- What brought you here?
- When did it first start?
- Has this happened before?
- When did you last feel like this?
- What are you feeling like right now?

Use of techniques

Body tension exercise

- Where is the tension in your body?
  Focus on thTe tension, make it worse.
- Let your mind float. What comes to mind?
  REPEAT – encouraging the client to 'get smaller and smaller'.

(This exercise will be shown in more detail in a later chapter.)

Anniversaries

- Is this date/day important? Did anything dramatic occur around this time last year/previous years – (e.g., death/abortion/break-up of relationship)?

Loss

- Have you lost a loved one recently/Has anyone died recently/Have you had a broken relationship?

Awareness of world events

- How is the war affecting you and your family?
- How is the recession affecting you and your family?

Awareness of the client's context and change

- What major changes have occurred lately (e.g., child gone to school/leaving home/being unemployed/ becoming a student/getting a promotion/moving house/exams)?
- Is there anyone close to you in hospital/ill?

Heimler social functioning theory

- What balance of positives and negatives is there in main areas of life – work/finance /family (primary/ secondary)/feelings about self.

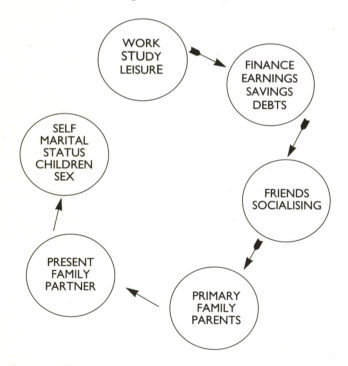

Figure 1. Progressive diagram of question areas inspired by the Heimler Social Functioning concept.

Practical considerations

● Are you eating/sleeping/relaxing?
  What is preventing you? (If relevant)

Listening to the music to find THE focus

Where is the emotion:

● in the voice?
● in the body?
● in the tears?
● What does the client say is the reason for coming to therapy?
● What does the client want?
● Does the client want to explore the focal area identified as carrying the emotion? If not, explore/challenge.

CHAPTER THREE

THE IMPORTANCE OF THE FIRST SESSION

The importance of the first session has already been mentioned briefly. The manner in which the first session is dealt with is *critical* to the shortening of the therapy. In particular the therapist should pay very careful attention to the client and to *every* detail of what happens in therapy, from the *very first moments of the encounter* with the client. This is essential to the brief approach and a very important factor in the shortening process.

Careful attention in the first moments

The words that the client uses in the opening sentences of the therapeutic encounter are crucial and often contain the kernel of the whole contract. Therefore, it is vital that the therapist notes every word that the client says in those first few minutes. Right from the moment that the therapist first encounters the client, the therapist needs to be paying very careful attention, to both what the client is saying and how they are saying it. If the client has actually stated why they have come or what it is that they want from the sessions once, they will feel that it has been said. They may then, quite reasonably, make the assumption that the therapist and they are on the same track. But this may not be the case.

Don't miss *the* moment

Often, clients will blurt out what they have come for in the first few minutes. At times therapists are too busy with their own agenda of, say, putting the client at their ease. For example, asking if they found the venue all right, explaining about confidentiality, and taking some factual information, name address, referral agent, etc. All of this may be done in the good intention of helping the client to relax and because the information is, indeed, required. These matters are important, but I suggest that some-times, in this process, something important can be lost. We may well overlook what the client is actually saying. We may miss the moment. One must avoid the first session being a kind of throw-away, warming-up, or intro-ductory session.

The sacred moment

Winnicott used to refer to the 'sacred moment'. He found that the children who were coming for therapy had been waiting perhaps some days for their appointment. They would rehearse what it was that they wanted to say and would blurt out why they had come in the first few moments. It is important not to lose this. An example of this is client F (Rawson, 2002, p. 184). I asked, 'What has brought you here?' Her answer: 'I've been depressed – well, since I was nine years old', gave the clue to the whole of her problem.

Intake sessions

In the light of what has been said about the first moments of a therapy session, I question the system of 'intake sessions', which is a very common way of working in counselling centres. This is where the client has already seen a therapist for assessment and is then referred on to the therapist who will continue to see them. Has the sacred moment then been lost? I suggest that it might have been. The intake or assessment worker needs to be very aware of the importance of those first moments. If this is not attended to, there is the real danger of the key first comments not being passed on in the summary that is given to the counsellor who is to see the client. The client, because they have said it once, whatever 'it' is, may not realize the necessity of saying it all again to the new person. There can, then, be an important gap in the proceedings. It is not insurmountable. The issues will no doubt reappear at a later stage since, as Patrick Casement observes, 'the clients give us prompts – all sorts of them' (2004, p. 15). In this way the client does, in a manner of speaking, supervise the therapist. If, however, we want to keep therapy as short as possible, then we need to avoid the necessity of this happening and to be tuned in from the first moment. In this way the sacred moment will not be lost and the true work of the therapy begins straight away, arising out of these key first words.

Find a way to recreate a 'first session'

Where there is an intake and referral-on system, we need to find a way to ensure that we *do* know exactly why the client has come for therapy. Even if the therapist has been given very accurate notes from the intake worker, the therapist needs to satisfy themselves that they and the client are working on the same issues. I think it is helpful to almost recreate a first session. One has to make sure that the client does not feel as if they are just repeating things that they have already said to the intake worker and are getting nowhere. The therapist might approach this from the following angle: 'Since some time has elapsed now since you saw the assessment worker, perhaps you could fill in what was going on for you at that time and what the situation is now.' Or one might say something like: 'I know that you have spoken already to the intake worker and they have passed on to me a summary of your conversation, as they told you they would, but I would find it most helpful if you could tell me in your own words what made you decide to come for therapy, so that I can be quite sure I have understood what it is that you are seeking from the sessions.'

The beginning of therapy

In the brief approach, session one is very much the beginning of the therapy. The therapist will endeavour to be very focused as to what their client wants and expects from therapy. They will attempt to tease out the issues and to pin down their client to gain clarity as to the issues. This process of clarification helps both client and therapist and ensures that both are working on the same issues. In this process the therapy begins from the first moments of the encounter and one can be working at depth from this first session, utilizing any appropriate skills. The client often tries, whether consciously or unconsciously, to avoid the real and painful issue. At times, as a defence, the client will talk of issues that are not really where the pain is. The therapist's task is gently to help them to have sufficient confidence in the situation to dare to reveal the real issue. It is the therapist's task to help the client to open up in this way. Observation of the client's body language will often reveal where the real issue is. It is important that the therapist stays where the emotion is even if the discussion is moving in another direction. The emotion is in the now and is of paramount importance. For example, client Oliver rattled off a number of issues that he wanted to speak about, so many that I wrote them down. Then I read them back to him, asking him which he wished to start on. As I read there was one where I observed tears welling in his eyes, but he did not choose that one to discuss. I gently queried the fact that he had not chosen the one that seemed to be upsetting him most and suggested that, really, this one might be the most helpful for him to explore with me. The tears once again welled and he began to share the painful area with me.

Touching the pain

At times one session may be enough. There are some practitioners who work as 'one session therapists' and produce good results. One aspect of the first session that is of prime importance is to touch the client's pain. In doing this the client is given hope that the therapist knows where the pain is, that they can handle it, and that it is not going to destroy the therapist. In touching on the sore spot, painful as that might be, the opening up is already begun and the healing process is started. In touching the pain we are also letting the client know that we can bear it. It is not going to destroy us. The client needs to know this and one can often be aware of the client testing us out as therapists. Almost like dipping a toe in the water:

Is the therapist going to hear me?
Is the therapist going to be alert to my clues?
Is the therapist going to be shocked, or judge, or preach.
Will they know what to do?
Can they handle my problem?
Can they bear my pain?

It is hoped that by the end of the first session the client will feel that the therapist has understood their issue and will have the hope that they will be helped with it.

Table 1 provides a useful summary of the many aspects to be borne in mind in the first session (see the quick reference notes, p. 64).

The first session needs to begin the therapy

The first session is indeed an introductory session and one in which the therapist and client get to know each other and about the process of therapy. It may be good, for instance, to allow a few minutes at the start of a session to help the client to 'arrive' and to get off their chest anything that is impeding them from going straight into the work of the contract. For example, if they have just witnessed a road traffic accident on their way to the therapist's office, they may well need to offload about this before getting down to the issues they booked the appointment for. Even if such a need is apparent, the therapist needs to continue to be fully alert and to be noting exactly what is said and how it is said and to very quickly focus on the client's reason for being there. To do this one might say something along the following lines: 'As you know we only have a limited number of sessions. Are you ready to continue with what we had decided to work on or would you prefer to spend some time talking about the impact of the accident on you?' The therapist and client then come to a decision about what the focus of this session is to be. If the witnessed accident is clearly more prominent in the client's mind than their original issue this is likely to become the focus.

Negotiating and renegotiating the contract

This process of negotiation and renegotiation is a feature of the brief approach. We need to be very much in tune with where the client is, and the work of therapy needs to be explicitly agreed. So, such renegotiation of the contract may occur more than once within the course of a brief contract, or even in a session. For example, if the client, in becoming more focused on their issues, realizes that their presenting issue was masking a deeper one, the deeper one then becomes the focus of the work.

Setting the end from the beginning

When a short-term contract with a client begins, the brevity of the contract is pointed out. We highlight the limited time available and begin the countdown. We are setting the end from the beginning, which is one of the shortening factors in the approach.

Countdown of sessions

Even from the first session the client needs to be aware of the countdown of sessions, as this puts a certain urgency into the situation, and reminds them that they need to bring to the fore whatever is bothering them. There is no time for procrastination.

Brief group therapy

This brief contract work can be undertaken with a group also. Eight sessions seems to work well for groups.

In this instance, over a period of days before the group starts, each member of the group is seen individually for half an hour by the group leader. This is to acertain what it is that each one wants from the sessions. Together they get to a point where there is one sentence to sum up what the client wants to achieve in the eight sessions. This will be shared in the group at the first session, each member of the group reading out what it is that they want to achieve by the time the group contract ends. In this way all the group members can help each other to reach their objectives. I have surprised even myself at how much one can achieve in the half-hour pre-group contracting session. One has to be extremely focused, active, and incisive, and both the client and therapist need to be aware of the time limit for this session, i.e., half an hour. It is this half-hour that begins the work of the therapy. I believe that it should be undertaken by the therapist who is to lead the group.

Starting therapy at a sprint

This chapter has stressed the need to start the work of therapy at a sprint, with the therapist being intensely alert to the client from the very first moments of the encounter. The first session thus begins the work of therapy, it is not just an introductory session. Having stressed the importance of the first session, in the next chapter I say a little more about the focus, that central facet of brief therapy.

QUICK REFERENCE NOTES

Initial interview in short-term focal therapy

The following is an example of a first interview with a client:

(1) 'What made you decide to come for counselling?'
(Expect to discover the referral agent, precipitating event, desire for change, expectations of what therapy can offer.)

(2) 'What do you expect from counselling/hope to achieve from the counselling sessions?'
(This is an opportunity to bring unrealistic expectations down to earth. There are no magic answers, we facilitate the clients' search for their own answers using our facilitative skills. This is an opportunity to outline the method of therapy here, e.g., talking about the situation, getting in touch with feelings, looking for links with the past, etc.)

(3) 'How will you measure your success in relation to the therapy?' For example, a male client wanting to improve confidence in relation to girls might see inviting a fellow student he likes to a coffee as a measure of success – i.e., a limited, achievable specific goal.

(4) 'How do you feel about this situation now that you have taken this important step? Do you want to ask me anything about the process?'
(The therapist may outline here a little more about the counselling process in terms of contract, number of sessions, frequency of meetings, etc.)

(5) The therapist:
- checks if the client still wants to continue
- confirms what they are both working on

- summarizes the general focus
- obtains agreement as to accuracy and joint contract and concludes the session.

(For example, in this summing up, the therapist will draw on material noted in the answers to the early questions, such as the desire for change, how the client and therapist will know they've succeeded in their goal, what the general focal issue is. Often it is the opening few words that give the clue for this.)

These questions are examples only. The flexibility, experience, and instinct of the therapist in relationship with the client dictates the format and the language that can elicit the necessary information to fulfill the aims.

Aims of initial interview

1.

The aim is that the client:

    (a) leaves with a clearer idea as to what therapy is all about;

    (b) has established a rapport with the therapist;

    (c) is clearer as to the problem area;

    (d) has a feeling of being listened to, and that the therapist has understood the nature of the problem as shown by accurate empathy and summary;

    (e) has hope, since the limited contract implies that movement can occur quite quickly;

    (f) has a feeling of being 'contained' but not 'constrained' by the limited contract.

2.

The aim is that the therapist has:

    (a) established a relationship with the client;

    (b) a clear idea as to the focal area to be explored;

    (c) established a 'working alliance' with the client;

    (d) a contract in terms of focus;

    (e) agreed the time frame for the contract.

Table 1. Important aspects of the first session as seen from the research case work.

(a) The client's assessment of the situation

(i)   Learning what therapy is
(ii)   Testing out the therapist and the therapy situation
(iii)   Deciding if it's trustworthy
(iv)   Deciding if it meets their needs
(v)   Giving clues

(b) The therapist's role in the situation is:

(i)   Teaching what therapy is
(ii)   Demonstrating what therapy is by getting started
(iii)   Enlisting the adult as co-therapist
(iv)   Helping the client to become their own therapist
(v)   Dealing with the defences
(vi)   Recognizing the client's pain and issue and communicating this
(vii)   Assessing if client is suitable for therapy, ie. is the client motivated/insightful/able to relate/has an issue to work through.

(c) The joint task

(i)   Client and therapist seeking and finding the focus
(ii)   Client and therapist agreeing to the contract in relation to the focal issue and the number of sessions

---

Source: Rawson, 2002, p. 192, Table VII.

CHAPTER FOUR

JOINTLY AGREED STRATEGIC FOCUS: CONTRACT PART I

In this chapter I return to importance of the focus in brief therapy and of holding the client to the focus. I also elaborate on the idea of the strategic focus.

The focus in session two and onwards

Earlier in the book I have outlined ways to find the focus in the first session. In subsequent sessions it is important to allow the the client a little time to say where they are since the last meeting, to 'arrive' and to get off their chest anything that is impeding them from going straight into the work of the contract. This might simply be done by asking if they are ready to continue with the agreed contract or whether there is something more pressing on their minds. I usually allow a client up to ten minutes for this, if needed, and then would check whether we stay with the new topic or continue with the previously agreed work. They may be quite ready to go on straight away with the contract, and some do continue almost as if the previous session were five minutes ago. For others, the events of the week may be powerfully acting on their lives and distracting from the focus. By checking if these now are preferred as the focus, or whether it is appropriate to continue where we left off, we become focused once more.

On becoming more focused

Therapists who have experimented with being more focused and with attending more to the very first words of their clients often find that things move more quickly than they had formerly thought possible. Therapists have said, for example:

> 'My client has achieved more than I would have believed possible in just one session.'

> 'I couldn't believe how deep we were going so soon.'

> 'I dared to be more challenging than I would normally be and kept the client very focused.'

> 'I really must share with the group about my client whom I have seen for several months. I checked at the start of the session whether we were focusing on the issues that she felt she needed to. This set her off on a different tack altogether. She opened up far more than she had done previously and some really painful issues emerged that she had not mentioned before.'

> 'Several of my clients decided that it was time to leave therapy soon. I felt that this was something to do with the course but was not really conscious of having done anything different.'

Holding the focus

A while ago I went to see the well known pair, Torville and Dean, performing their dances on ice. While there and enjoying the performance I observed the way that the spotlight followed the couple wherever they went around the skating rink. This prompted me to reflect about an aspect of brief therapy: the focus. The spotlight keeps the dancers in focus the whole time. The operator of the light ensures that the beam follows them round the rink; their every movement and twist and turn kept in the spotlight, they are never allowed to drift out of that focus into obscurity.

In the same way the therapist needs to keep the agreed focal area in mind the whole time.

Synchronicity

There are other elements of Torville and Dean's performance that I mused upon also in relation to brief therapy. It demonstrates synchronicity, mirroring, absolute togetherness and complementarity. These are all parallels for brief therapy and, indeed, any therapy.

Zooming in

The skating performance was also on the closed circuit television. My musings continued as I observed the camera zooming in on different aspects of the couple, giving close-up views of them. At one time the camera zoomed in and focused on the intricate footwork, at another on the couple's faces, and so on. Then the camera would shift once more to the overall picture, still holding the couple in the spotlight but showing their full figures, as they went at considerable speed around the rink. Only at the end of the performance did the camera take in the wider scene, with some shots of the audience to put the whole scene in context.

What a superb analogy for the way focused therapy can work. There is the overall focus, which is kept in mind the whole time, but as we work with the client on this we focus on different aspects of it, examining these in detail. Then it is all related to the main heading or focus that has been agreed. Periodically, the main focus is also related to the overall picture and how it fits in with the rest of the client's life.

The strategic focus

The issue of focus is so central to the approach of brief psychodynamic therapy that more needs to be said about it. We have already seen some of the ways to home in on the key issue for the client and to hold the client to this. We endeavour not to get distracted into exploring irrelevant sidetracks and if seemingly unrelated issues come in, then we check how these relate to the contract. The contract is the agreement as to what we are working on with the client and the time scale that we agree to work to. More will be said about contract in the Chapter Five.

The strategic focus is where the present and past pain is. This will be apparent in the emotion shown by the client, in the body language, in the atmosphere in the room, or, at times, in the therapist's own body awareness.

The client usually has a sense of where the real issues lie. However, they do not always reveal these to the therapist straight away. As we said when looking at the importance of the first session, there is often a certain testing out of the therapist. *Will they understand my pain? Can they cope with my pain? Will they know what to do? Will they pick up my hints?* Sometimes, intentionally or unintentionally, the client will give us a focus that masks the real issue. It is part of our task to enable them to bring the strategic issue to the surface, the one that is at the heart of the problem. At times clients will try to talk about an absent other. This is of relevance only if it aids the client in response to that other. It is the client's trip and no one else's.

I have occasionally heard supervisors and therapists discussing their clients, saying, for example: 'I really think he/she needs to do more work on x or y or z. and I think she/he is acting this way because of a or b or c.' While, perhaps, there is a place for such speculation in training as examples of what might be going on, we need to be very careful to facilitate our *client's* trip and not allow it to become an interesting exercise for the therapist. Also, we need to limit the work we do with a client to what they wish to explore. That is not to limit the therapist's freedom to challenge and to reflect blind spots of the clients to them, this as a challenge to encourage them, possibly, to explore wider issues, and simply to stress the need to keep the client's needs as the focus.

Roots in the past

Once the strategic focus has been narrowed down and both therapist and client are clear about it, the therapist also needs to help the client to see that this may have its roots in the past, since this is where the problem probably comes from. Louis Marteau refers to this underlying problem as the 'nuclear crisis' – i.e., stemming from an emotional crisis in childhood (Marteau, 1986, p. 81).

He also observes that

> If this presenting crisis is truly nuclear, then getting it out at the roots must be the aim of the therapy while the process will be to reach through the present crisis to grasp the very roots. This means that the presenting crisis needs to be the major focus through which we will attain the roots. The true resolution of the presenting crisis, which means reaching the roots, will be the test of the successful outcome. [*ibid.*]

Renegotiation

At times, the focus that we initially agree upon turns out not to be the most important issue to explore. If this is the case then a process of renegotiation of the contract needs to take place. This can happen for all sorts of reasons. Perhaps the client has been testing us and now wants to look at the real issue. Perhaps life circumstances have changed and now something in the new situation is more pressing. Maybe the client had not realized that one topic had masked a more serious and strategic problem. The important thing is that client and therapist are clear about and are in agreement as to what they are working on, jointly agreeing a change of contract if that is what is required.

Refocusing

At other times, it is not a change of contract that is required but a refocusing on what has already been agreed. Sometimes we need to get the client back on course, perhaps by reminding them what the contract was, or maybe asking how the topic now being talked about relates to what they came for. Also, it is good to keep the time limit before the client and point out the need to prioritize in order to achieve what they want in the time agreed.

Homework

One of the elements of brief therapy is the use of 'homework'. Some people dislike that word because of its connotations with school. Essentially, we encourage the client to work on their issues in some way at home in order to speed up the process. Clearly, in relation to the rest of a person's life, the traditional fifty-minute hour is very little. Therefore, if the client can give a little time throughout the week to their issues, great progress can be made in a short time. It also encourages the client to 'become their own therapist', which is another aspect of the method. Thus, they take with them into the rest of their life the skills that they learn in the therapy situation.

One example of how this might work from early on is if the client is having trouble narrowing down what they want of the therapy. There may be several issues that are bothering them. 'At home work' in this instance might be to ask the client to think about all the different things they want to cover and to select the one or possibly two that they would like to focus on in the next session. The therapist should encourage them to choose the one they most want help with, in view of the brief nature of this type of work. It is worth pointing out that it is often the most painful one that is most important to look at. Sometimes more than one of the issues will be selected by the next session. It is relevant to hear why the client has chosen the two and often it becomes apparent that in some way they interlink with each other. The client usually has a pretty good idea about what they want from therapy, even if initially they have difficulty in verbalizing it. Asking the clients to be specific helps them to begin to tackle the issue and keeps them thinking and working on their issues between sessions. Often a great deal can change in the course of the week.

Homework needs to be integrated into the work of the session and to arise from what has gone on there. It can be thought about with the client. It may be a suggestion made by the therapist or can be very open-ended, e.g., 'It might be helpful to think a bit more about that during the week'. More is said about homework in Chapter Seven. The quick reference notes suggest some homework for the therapist!

The focus that we have examined further above and the time limit are negotiated with the client to form a contract for the work of therapy. In the following chapter we examine further the importance of time limits in brief therapy.

QUICK REFERENCE NOTES

Fixing the focus

1. Fixing the focus

- Agree contract and focal area, i.e., not just the 'now' area, but how this links with the past. For instance, at the point where the emotion is, help client to reflect on similar feelings from earlier times, e.g., (to a client grumbling about the boss) 'Is that how Dad treated you?' 'That sounds like a small child's reaction.' 'How are you feeling in relation to me here and now and we talk about this?'

- Homework to think about the work of the session and about the agreed focal area, or, if the focus not yet clear and agreed , to think about the work of the session and see if by the next session they can be more specific as to what they want from therapy and what they wish to focus on.

2. Holding the focus

CLIENT/THERAPIST AGREEMENT AS TO
THE FOCUS IS ALWAYS REQUIRED

At the start of the session allow time for client to talk
about issues on the surface and predominating since the
last session, readjusting the focus if necessary; e.g., if
agreed focus is break-up of a relationship but since last
week a close relative has died, focus probably needs to
shift to that *if the client wants to do so.*

If the agreed focus stands then work can begin after a
few minutes, e.g., 'We were going to talk about . . .'

REACHING THROUGH THE GENERAL FOCUS

Going deeper, e.g., if the focus is about difficulty in
developing equal relationships, how does it relate to the
childhood?

ZOOMING IN

Be alert for any opportunity to 'home in' on the focal
issue, e.g., if the client says, 'I feel depressed', some questions to ask are as follows:

When do you feel depressed?
When was the last time you felt that way?
Give me an example.
Tell me more about that.
What happened?
Where were you?
Who was there?

What were you doing?
What were you feeling?
What did you want to do?
How old do you feel as you tell me about that? How old
    were you? How old are you?

N.B. Change of tense in the question can move the client
into a childhood/past memory or feeling.

THERAPIST'S ROLE TO HOLD THE BOUNDARIES

- to hold the focus – once agreed
- to facilitate client's search for meaning re the issue
- to facilitate the client's dealing with unfinished business and emotions
- to facilitate the client's applying their learning to their
  lives
- to facilitate the changing patterns of behaviour and
  habits

THERAPIST USES A VARIETY OF SKILLS
FLEXIBLY

- Tone of voice
- Silence
- Empathic response
- Emoting
- Challenge
- Gestalt/fantasy/questions/observations/body work,
  etc
- education, e.g., grief symptoms

The focal therapist makes particular use of selective
inattention/selective attention/selective neglect /selective
follow-up.

The strategic focus

That is the issue where the present and past *pain* is, i.e., tears, silence, body language, weight of emotion in the room.

- Where the client's reflective instinct dictates the focus to be.

- Where the therapist's own body awareness picks up the client's emotions – if these are agreed by the client.
- When the client's body language shifts towards the therapist.
- It is the client's *choice* of focus – the therapist's task is to highlight possibilities by reflecting back to the client and then to hold the focus once agreed.
- The focus could be a mutual search for the focus or key to the depression/anxiety, etc., within an agreed time limit. The time limit will help the strategic issue/focus to emerge – probably in the penultimate session.
- The focus needs to be related to the *client's* blocks, feelings, awarenesses in relation to his or her world. Exploring the motivations or psychopathology of an absent 'other' may be of relevance, but only if it aids the client in *his/her* response to that other.

Aspects of brief therapy to practise (homework)

- Be more aware of reaching a clear focus in the first session.
- Agree the number of sessions with the client.
- Be more aware of where the emotion is in the first session.

Questions for the therapist to think about in relation to the focus

Therapist task

The aim of the therapist is to find and fix the focus, helping the client to be very specific and teasing out exactly what it is that they want to work on.

> Have I avoided getting sidetracked?
> Have I enlisted the client's co-operation in this search for the focus?
> Have I negotiated the time frame for the sessions and have we agreed the number?
> Have I picked up the clues and homed in on key emotional issues whether verbal or non-verbal?
> Have I been afraid to begin the therapeutic work in the first session even though convinced that the therapeutic alliance has been clearly established?

CHAPTER FIVE

JOINTLY AGREED TIME SCALE: CONTRACT PART II

The importance of the jointly made contract re focus and time

In brief therapy one of the elements that helps to speed the process is the making of a contract. This is worked out jointly with the client and therapist. The contract includes three essential elements: the focus, the time scale, and the joint agreement about both of them. The focus has already been looked at in some detail in earlier chapters, and the joint nature of the work of brief therapy also. Here, I explore more about the time aspect. Those who wish to explore the aspect of contract in more depth might wish to consult Rawson, 2002, pp. 137–158.

Time/number of sessions

How long should the contract be? For those readers who come from a long-term therapy background, I am aware that there may be some resistence to the idea of brief work, although the fact that you are reading this is perhaps sign of openness to the concept. I find the following exercise is quite useful.

Time exercise

I wonder how you would feel if asked, say at a training group, to do the following exercise. This exercise is one that is quite often used to heighten our awareness and sensitivity to disabled issues and also as an exercise in trust. You are asked to pair up. One then would be blindfolded and the other would be asked to lead their partner around and to experience this situation for *10 minutes*. What would be your reaction? Usually, if I do this in a training session, most in the group are horrified at the time scale and the whole exercise and are wondering if they can keep it up for that time and what is the point, etc. They are much relieved when I say they do not to have to do it! I then ask them to be very aware of what they *feel* as I go on to the next exercise. I suggest you try it, too. I repeat the above, but say we will do it for just *one minute*. In the feedback that follows they are all much more positive; even if they can't see the point they are prepared to go along with it for that short time as it feels manageable and the issues of trust also seem more possible for that length of time. Some have quite strong and visible reactions to both ideas, but all are much more relaxed with the short one.

This exercise, I believe, may help the reader to be a little in touch with how some clients may feel about the brief time and to see it in a positive light.

The contract time limit

How does this relate to the client and the contract? As we explore the issue of how long should the contract be, I am aware that many therapists fear that the client will think that a few number of sessions will not be long enough for the client to resolve their problem. But, in fact, many clients are much relieved to know that the contract might be short. It is cheaper for one thing. It is less of a disruption to their lives, as coming for counselling surely is, and it inspires hope that they may be out of their pain soon.

Having a time limit provides the client with a certain safety and perhaps allows them to open up because it is only for a little while. There is a certain pressure, if there is only a little time, that pushes the client to think 'I'd better get on with it'. There is an aspect of loss that is both a positive and negative thing. The good side of it is the idea that they can get on with their life and, hopefully, feel better soon. The less good side is that they are losing their good relationship with the therapist. That can be noted and brought into the sessions. Often, the ending of the therapy contract brings back other losses. There is dependence upon the therapist even though the contract is brief; this is almost a necessary part of the trusting process. It is limited, though, by the knowledge that the end is there right from the beginning. We will look further at the issue of loss later on.

Spacing and length of sessions

The number of sessions and spacing of sessions for the contract needs to be agreed with the client. This may take the form of a certain number of sessions or a period of time. The sessions do not have to be on a weekly basis. In fact, a fortnightly gap can suit some people very well, time seems to go so quickly. The gap allows sufficient time for the client to have put into practice any aspect of homework that arose from the session. (We return to the concept of homework later in more detail.) In an Employee Assistance Programme (EAP) I worked with in Somerset, many of the clients opted for fortnightly sessions, if given the choice. There is nothing sacrosanct about the weekly session except, I would suggest, custom and practice. Equally, the same could be said of the fifty-minute hour or hour sessions, another tradition. Again in the Somerset practice, where either therapist or client travelled maybe four hours return to get to the venue of the session, a longer session at less frequent intervals made sense in terms of economy of time. The therapeutic work did not seem to be disadvantaged by this. I believe that there are also some therapists who practise a kind of marathon session of several hours in one go. I do not know enough about that to express an opinion of its effectiveness. I, personally, would be unable to concentrate for more than a couple of hours in one stretch. Although supervision is a different exercise from therapy, I find the hour and a half sessions that most of my supervisees opt for a very good span of time, in terms of both allowing a lot of content to emerge and concentration.

Having challenged assumptions a little here, most therapists still prefer the hour, or fifty-minute hour, sessions, and that applies to the brief psychodynamic model too. Sessions can be organized in other formats. They can be tapered off, for example, maybe three sessions on a weekly basis and then a follow-up session three weeks later. It can be appropriate to take account of public holidays, such as Christmas or Easter, or term times as the deadline, and then work out how to space sessions up to that time. I tend to offer four sessions and then a review. At the same time I sow the seed of the idea that probably four or six will be sufficient, since that is what most of the clients tend to choose. The time is specified along with the focus, so that we can say something along the lines of 'We will look at *x* for *y* weeks and then see where we have got'. This approach is less rigid than some brief models, for example, Mann's (1973), where twelve sessions are offered rigidly and much is made of the cut-off point. There is mileage in letting the client think that there is a definite cut-off point, i.e., only four or six sessions. This enables us to harness the deadline effect best. It is not necessary for the client to know initially that more sessions are available if they are needed. It is enough that the therapist knows this. However, I have found with most of my clients that the more flexible approach, where the client does know that more sessions can be negotiated if needed, works equally well and I prefer to work in this way. This more flexible approach to the number of sessions relies more heavily on the joint aspect of the decision. Given the statistics that I have cited elsewhere, the number of sessions still tends to average around four to six. This is true, even when my clients are fully aware that more sessions will be available, if they need them. I tend now to make a rigidly fixed ending only with clients who seem poorly motivated or who want to procrastinate, or ones who have great difficulties with letting go and with loss. A firm cut-off point can bring these deeper loss issues to the fore and they can then become the work of the sessions, if this is appropriate.

Interruptions

Interruptions are quite acceptable in this approach. By that I mean that we might work with a client on a particular issue for, say, four sessions. This being satisfactorily tackled, the client then goes on their way to assimilate the learning from this work for a number of weeks. Later they may return to explore a further issue. In long-term work much the same process happens, except that the client will continue to attend sessions with the therapist during the assimilation period. Learning tends to happen in peaks, and then there is a plateau stage as we come to terms with new concepts or practise new ways of responding to situations. In the brief approach, the client works in the plateau stage on their own. This is cheaper for them and does not encourage the dependence on the therapist that is the case in longer term work. The comparison is made, not to get into a debate about which is better or worse, but simply to highlight the difference and some of its consequences. In fact, is this not how we work with physical problems? We go to the doctor when there is something specifically wrong. That is treated and we don't go near the doctor until some other matter causes us a problem.

I referred earlier to the energy required in this method. I think that if this energy is lacking in the initial phase of therapy the therapy can tend to slip into a different mode, a slower and more ponderous one that will probably extend it. All is not lost if this happens; one simply needs to review with the client, see if we are achieving what the client wants, and refocus. Then we are able to proceed to work at the agreed focus and pace.

The dynamics of the deadline

There is a deadline effect induced by the limited contract. We will all have memories of times when we rushed to meet a deadline, whether it was an essay, or collecting the children from school, or catching a train or plane. A deadline has the effect of concentrating the mind wonderfully. We become very focused on the task in hand. We ignore anything that does not pertain to the goal to be reached by the set time. This is called 'selective inattention' if we apply it to brief therapy. How many of us have taken our time preparing, perhaps for an evening out? If we are unexpectedly invited out, with only a little time to get ready, we surely manage it in a very short time. Are we any more ready, or have we just speeded up the preparation?

The agreed number and spacing of sessions provides a kind of safety and containment, as well as a little pressure. The clients knows where they stand. This also has an economic angle since, if the client is contracted for six sessions to work on their strategic issue, they can work out the cost. While there are no guarantees as to outcome, there can be a reasonable expectation of progress. The short number of sessions also inspires hope. If the therapist thinks it can be dealt with in that time, it can't be that terrible.

You will recall that in an earlier chapter I placed emphasis on the therapist believing in the method. Some centres offer a brief contract initially, but then put their clients on a waiting list for 'proper' therapy, i.e., long-term. This type of approach militates against brief therapy being effective.

The end from the beginning

In the brief approach we need reminders of the end from the beginning and can almost count down to the end session by session. For example, 'This is session four, so we have two more to complete the work you wanted to in that time. We will need to allow some time for review in the last session.' Often a great deal emerges in the penultimate session. Or we might say on day one. 'We have four sessions and have decided that we are looking at *x*, so where would you like to begin?'

Joint nature of brief therapy

In brief therapy it is important for client and therapist to work together to find and fix the focal area and the number of sessions involved for this. They need to arrive jointly at the contract by finding the focus and agreeing the time scale. In the process of doing this the therapist needs to avoid getting sidetracked. The client, who will no doubt be giving clues as to their problem, may also offer some resistance and throw in some red herrings. This was shown in the table summarizing what goes on in the first session. Such red herrings can be part of the testing out of the therapist by the client. The client, so to speak, is wondering: *Will the diversion be noticed? Can they stand my pain? Are they able to tell the wood from the trees?*

When the therapist picks the client up on a deviation and brings them back to the focus, the client may actually feel relieved and begins to trust the therapist more. The client in this situation feels held, listened to, taken seriously, given hope, excited. The therapist may be amazed at the amount of material that comes up in just a short time, even in the first session.

High energy therapy

Therapists working with this more interventionist approach are aware of high energy levels. It is an active approach. You may recall the sprinter analogy referred to earlier. Therapists express surprise that very deep material surfaces so quickly, and that the level of trust is also established so quickly. Their fears that the client will be opened up and then abandoned seem to dissipate as they find that, since both client and therapist know of the time limits, both are working to have a proper closure. In fact, the client is not left all open and raw and should not be.

Effect of time limit on therapist

Many therapists new to the brief approach say how good it is to have 'permission to get cracking and to move the session along', which this tradition gives, since it feels natural to them. Previously they have held back because being so active was not allowed by their particular tradition of therapy. In beginning the therapeutic work more quickly than they would previously have dared to do, they have found it worked well.

The approach is not rigid

In the above we have examined the aspect of time in the contract and the joint nature of the contract has been stressed once more. More than once the idea of renegotiation has come up, emphasizing that the therapist and the approach is not rigid. The approach discussed here is one that expects the therapist to be flexible in many respects, and this flexibility is the subject of Chapter Six.

QUICK REFERENCE NOTES

Time limited psychotherapy

The limited contract

(i)   Fixed number of sessions.
(ii) Agreed circumscribed focal area.

(i) The fixed number of sessions provides the following for the client:

- Safety, e.g., 'It'll be over soon.'
- Containment, e.g., 'The real feelings can be allowed out because it's only for a little while.'
- Hope, e.g., 'If the therapist thinks they can help in six sessions it can't be so bad after all.'
- Pressure, e.g., 'I've only got four/eight sessions so I'd better get on with it/say it.' 'I'd better work between sessions to get the most out of the therapy hour.'
- Loss: anticipation of the last session from the beginning.
- Independence (positive), e.g., 'I can leave all this behind soon.'
- Independence (negative), e.g. 'I can't cope with the loss.' This can be turned to positive as the focus becomes that of dealing with loss/past losses/echoes.
- Dependence (positive), e.g., 'It's only a short time so I can lean on the therapist for a while.'
- Dependence (negative), e.g., 'It's not long enough.' The focus needs to deal with what does 'not enough' mean and with loss/past echoes/losses/neediness.

N.B. A new contract can be made at the therapist's discretion and various ways of being flexible can be used to suit client need.

Flexibility is based on experience/instinct and negotiation with the client is required.

(ii) The circumscribed focal area

- Agreed general focus – concentrates the mind of client and therapist.
- Provides a backcloth – triggers appropriate/related material for the client.
- Provides direction – enables the client to achieve the original goal.
- Avoids client/therapist getting lost in interesting side-tracks.
- Under the microscope – allows sufficient time for all the detail in one incident/ issue to be investigated
- Microcosm – contains elements of other conflict/ problems. Patterns emerge.
- Strategic focus – may emerge through examination of general focus. Through this to the past pattern or event.

NB: Flexibility required of the therapist. Focus can be renegotiated with client as appropriate – or the material brought back to the original agreed focus. Experience/ instinct/and negotiation are necessary.

The dynamics of the deadline

Which of us is not familiar with the effect of the deadline? The assignment date for the student, the committee meeting where one has to have read certain reports, the check-in time at the airport or station, these are all familiar events to most of us. Such events have a remarkable way of concentrating the mind and energy. We tend to focus on the essentials that will achieve the desired end. The student abandons the longer term academic projects and other tasks to focus on whatever is necessary to meet the immediate deadline. The committee member perhaps closes the door on those making demands to concentrate on the report, and so on.

In therapy, the same deadline effect can operate. Which counsellor or therapist has not seen a client make rapid strides in the limited time available before emigrating or leaving the area? Would the same people have reached such a satisfactory position in such a short time if they had had no 'deadline' in sight?

In college counselling/therapy sessions, the deadline is built in by term ends, by exams, industrial placements, and holidays. In more general settings, events such as moving jobs or house can end sessions.

How many therapists deliberately capitalize on the 'endings' effect? Those who do report the remarkable strides clients make in very few sessions.

Those therapists who contract a limited number of sessions and keep careful note of the pattern of work may notice the particular importance of the sessions nearing the 'deadline'.

The number of sessions to produce considerable change can be so few that many would be sceptical. Four to six sessions would be a reasonable span to achieve real change with many people when working focally, strategically, and psychodynamically.

'By mutual arrangement' (Rawson, 1995)

Focal therapy is a psychotherapy approach where client and therapist work together on an agreed focal area of the client's life. They do this within an agreed and limited time-span.

The 'focal area' is negotiated. Often clients present an initial problem which is bothering them. This may then become the initial general focus of the sessions. However, as exploration goes ahead, it may become apparent that there is an underlying problem relating to the initial focus. This will then become the specific focus of the remaining sessions of the contract.

The term 'contract' is used because in this approach the mutual agreement as to the focus of the sessions is important. Once client and therapist have agreed on the general area to be explored, it is then the therapist's task to ensure that this happens. If it becomes apparent that the agreed focal area is no longer relevant, a revised contract is negotiated.

The clarity as to what the therapy is about serves to concentrate the minds and energy of both client and therapist. This is a particularly intense form of therapy and requires alert attention to every aspect of the therapeutic relationship.

Every word, expression, hesitation, body language and the emotional atmosphere need to be monitored carefully by the therapist. In so doing, important clues are gained to move the therapy on so that positive results are achieved.

The agreed time limit or limited number of sessions also concentrates mind and energy. It encourages client and therapist to stick to the point – and to selectively ignore material that has no bearing on the focus agreed. However, this does not mean that there will not be wide areas of the person's life referred to. What it does mean is that like a person creating a tapestry – every thread will be woven in to contribute to the original theme to make-up [*sic*] a complete picture so that any theme that emerges in the therapy session will be related to the overall agreed focus.

Since the clients are helped to clarify what it is they need from the therapy, they will thereby be helped to explore related areas of their lives. It is as if one is placing an aspect of life under a microscope. By obtaining a clear picture, the tangles and patterns can be clearly seen and unravelled.

The first step is to see clearly. This will not be simply a cognitive experience but will expect to touch on the emotions. In many cases, this will mean a reliving of a long-forgotten or deeply-buried painful experience. This remembering will be a cathartic experience – and a healing experience.

In this way, the focal therapy is seen as a psychodynamic approach. The client is encouraged to see/explore their problem in relation to any childhood links or past events. This remains focussed [*sic*] and relating to the present issue.

It is not thought necessary in this approach to go through the whole childhood but rather to focus on the issue still affecting the present. The 'unfinished business' belonging to the past will tend to lead people to patterns of behaviour that attempt to resolve the unfinished business – often in a maladaptive way. It may be this that unknowingly brings the client to therapy.

Maintaining the focus requires activity on the part of the therapist. Techniques such as gestalt, or fantasy or bodywork are used to move the sessions on.

At times, the client will show resistance to the work. One must remember that no one relishes the exploration of painful and traumatic areas, so such resistance is wholly understandable. It will be tackled by [the] therapist and brought immediately into the work of the session.

The resistance will be explored. The contract will be renewed – does the client want to work on the issues at this time or not? The choice is theirs. This challenge often galvanises the client into facing the difficult area.

If, however, the client decides to withdraw from therapy, this should not be seen as a failure on the part of either therapist or client. Rather, it indicates that this may not be the right time for the topic to be looked at.

It is important to remember that people have lives outside the 50 minutes per week when they see the therapist. Events may be impinging externally that make withdrawal from counselling expedient – for example, taking on a new job or sitting an exam. The day before such events would not be the time to open up old wounds from the past. Instinctively clients will know this and resist the therapist's attempts to facilitate their working on the agreed issues.

However, clients do not always think to alert their therapist to such external life factors. Therefore it is up to the therapist to check out, where possible, such mitigating [*sic*] circumstances.

Resistance might also reflect a kind of self-preservation response or an attempt not to disrupt the status quo. For example, the adult survivor of child abuse might be reluctant to continue therapy if the logical conclusion would be to expose the abuser. This might disrupt a whole family network of relationships that the survivor believes needs to remain intact.

Since this type of therapy is based on a therapeutic alliance of an agreed contract, such resistance can be talked about and explored. The work will either continue or cease – both by agreement. This involves activity on the part of the therapist and the ability to deal with both the client's anger and pain.

It is the therapist's task to 'pin down' the client. Sensitively but firmly, rather as a surgeon needs to be firm and incisive, the therapist needs to facilitate the client in exploring the area of pain.

Once the client decides to continue the work, the therapist needs to hold to the contract firmly and to move on. Such resistance may well indicate that they are close to the issue that is to be the most important of the session.

This is likely to be the most frightening and the most painful to the client. The client needs to be sure that the therapist is 'there' for them and that she can handle the situation. Some of the resistance may be about these issues. The client is attempting to seek reassurance that it is safe to explore with this therapist, that what is so terrifying will not destroy them both.

The time limit facilitates this process. There is not time to skirt round the issues. This therefore mobilises the efforts of the client to get through the resistance and to undertake the work seen to be necessary. That is, to talk about, and get in touch with, the emotional and painful events of their past or present.

The therapist's activity will draw on experience and a wide range of therapeutic interventions. The structure of the approach affords little time to waste – so if one avenue does not move things along, another can be tried. Each client draws different skills from the therapist's repertoire but these must be integrated into the therapist's way of work, not used haphazardly or artificially applied.

The analogy of horse and rider is perhaps appropriate here. A skilled rider will adapt to their mount, using their equestian skills flexibly – at one time, firm; at another, gentle.

Every horse will draw out a different response and needs a particular understanding and approach. The therapist needs such a flexible and adaptable approach to every client. Each individual therapeutic relationship is unique and it is in this uniqueness that the mystery of the therapy works.

CHAPTER SIX

FLEXIBILITY

It is important that the therapist can be flexible. This applies to techniques, to the time scale and to the possibility of renegotiating the contract in respect of both focus and time as necessary.

Pinpoint the issues

In holding the focus and working with the client we need to pinpoint the issues, help the client to discharge the emotions that reside with these, and help them to change the situation in the present. The reason for this is so that they can move forward somewhat more freely.

With one client there may be no need to do anything other than ask, 'What brought you to the counselling?' for it all to pour out clearly and lucidly. Another client may be barely able to get out a few disjointed thoughts as to their emotional state and the therapist needs to be able to help them, applying appropriate skills flexibly.

Education

The flexibility of the therapist is called into play in finding and holding the focus. One of the ways to do this is that of education. This is an area that is sometimes over-looked. I believe that we need to help clients to be aware of psychological processes, to teach them how to become their own therapists. For example, so many people are utterly ignorant as to the many effects that grief can have on them. Very often, once they are aware of this they no longer require therapy. I have so often heard clients say, 'Oh, I thought I was going mad. Now I understand what is happening, I think I can cope.'

The anniversary effect is particularly important for them to know about in relation to grief. See *Grappling with Grief* (Rawson, 2004, Chapter Three.)

Jacques

I cite Jacques as an example where a range of skills were required, including education. He is referred to in *Grappling with Grief* (Rawson, 2004). Jacques was an art student who was referred to me by one of his tutors because he had become aggressive suddenly and seemed utterly unable to produce any artwork. The tutor realized that there was something wrong, but Jacques was very reticent with him and would not open up about his problem. The tutor thought that the lad might speak more freely with someone who was not his tutor, who met him every day in class, and so brought Jacques to see me in the counselling service.

Jacques was French and was in this country for his course. He could speak and understand English, but this was not his first language. He would barely look at me and I gently suggested that it might help if he talked since clearly there was something that was bothering him.

So, here I was working with Jacques, a sixteen-year-old student who avoided my eye contact, who would only look at the floor, and who wouldn't say anything. I needed to establish some kind of rapport. I was sending signals of empathy and understanding, etc., non-verbally, but verbally I began to tell him about counselling and therapy and how it might help, and the sorts of things people came to therapy with. I refer to this as part of the educational role of the therapist. At intervals I would pause to see if he could tell me what was up and how I might help. He had decided to come for the appointment, so clearly did want help. I wondered if he might be able to draw whatever was troubling him, stressing that it need only be diagrammatic, not a great work of art. I indicated the pencils, felt tips, and paper on the coffee table between us. This resulted in some activity on his part. He took up the paper and began to draw. He chose a black felt tip. A rectangle appeared, then some grass around it, then it was heavily filled in, and then came the tombstone. When he had drawn that he put the paper down abruptly and, equally suddenly, got up and went to stand staring out of the window of my office. All this time he had not spoken and I had remained silent too, attempting to just be with him.

Not wanting to break the atmosphere in the room where I felt that he was reliving his pain and in some silent way allowing me to share it with him, I stayed silent. However, I went to the window and stood beside him, taking the picture he had drawn with me. After more minutes had passed silently I said, 'Someone close has died, haven't they?' Although there was no reply verbally, I understood that I was on the right track. Once again we shared a period of silence. 'Can you tell me about it?' I

101

asked quietly. I eventually gathered that it was his mother
who had died suddenly in France very recently. Once he
had managed to reveal that it was his mother who had
died the intense 'heavy' atmosphere in the room light-
ened. Jacques then went back to his chair and I returned
to mine. This profound silence had lasted for twenty
whole minutes. I cannot say what happened to him in
that period of time. I do know that I shared a very deep
experience within that silence with him and that it somehow moved him on with his grief. [Rawson, 2004, p. 18]

I was very 'present' to Jacques in the silence and I
believe that he was aware of my 'being fully with him' in
his pain.

In this example, then, I have, in addition to the normal
counsellor's repertoire of empathy, noting body language,
use of tone of voice, etc., employed the skills of education,
art therapy, and silence, as well as pertinent questions. I
also moved from the chair to be by him at the window. I
believe that this was important for him. I was there with
him, but silently, not intruding. Following Jacques and
myself returning to our respective chairs and his opening
up about the death of his mother, I spoke a little about
bereavement and its effects, thus educating once more,
this time about psychological processes. In doing this I
was attempting to normalize what he was feeling and
perhaps put what he was feeling into words and thus
make it more manageable. As we find in Shakespeare's
Macbeth Act IV. Sc.III:

'Give sorrow words: the grief that does not speak
Whispers the o'erfrought heart, and bids it break.'

After we had sat down again I spoke as follows:

many different reactions people have [to grief], including confusion, anger, and a loss of creativity, all of which he had been exhibiting in the classroom. I verbalized for him how sad he must be, and the pain he was in, and that it would get better, that his feelings on losing a loved one were normal and not to be frightened of. Our session ended with a much lighter feel. Jacques's hunched-up stance had now become more upright and open, and he was almost able to look at me and even managed a small smile as he went off. We made another appointment to see how things were going. By the next session he was no longer being aggressive in class and he was back to being able to get on with his creative work again. [Rawson, 2004, pp. 18–19]

The importance of 'being with' the bereaved

No doubt therapists are well aware of how important just *being with* the client in their pain of loss is. I also encourage those who are close to a person in grief to be aware of it, too. We often learn much from our clients; it was Jacques who taught me the this important lesson.

I would like to share with the reader . . . just how important 'presence' is to the one who is bereaved. It is not so much our words that can help but the being there with the person in their loss. So often people say I don't know what to say, but they do 'feel' for and with the person in their loss. This 'feeling' and awareness, empathy and support are tangible and can be of real help in the person's grief and loss. To stay present in the silence can be a gift any friend or companion can give to the bereaved. Obviously with sensitivity and to speak or not speak as appropriate. Sometimes, the friend who simply stays nearby the bereaved, reading their paper or who quietly gets on with some little job, can be a comfort. There, but not intruding. There, if called upon to share a memory or thought . . . [Rawson, 2004, p. 19]

Each client draws different skills from the therapist

Returning to flexibility, each client will draw different skills from the therapist appropriate to their particular case. Linda, in the example that follows, also needed a lot of help to be able to share her problem. Again we see a lot of silence and 'education' about counselling and therapy, but other skills also.

Linda

Linda came and slumped in the chair, looking at the floor. In response to my gentle questions, I got grunts, nods, or shakes of the head. I decided to explain a little more about how counselling works, i.e., that people who have something on their minds which is bothering them come and talk to a counsellor, who has no axe to grind, or judgement to make, but who will listen and help to clarify. I went on to explain how the therapist will use the skills they have learned to help the person come to terms with what is troubling them, or to express the emotions that they are bottling up. I explained how this can help the individual move on more freely and be able to get on with their life once more. I could tell that Linda was listening intently, but still she said nothing. I asked, 'Have you come of your own volition?', and I got a nod. 'Do you want to share something with me but don't know how?' Another nod. I decided to list a few of the problems that people bring. People come here with all sorts of problems and issues, relationship breakdowns, difficulties with parents, unwanted pregnancies, trouble with their tutors or with the course and their studies, assault, rape, or difficulties with flatmates, or a death. When I mentioned rape there was a tangible increase in the heaviness in the room that had been there since Linda came in. I went silent again and waited. I could feel a squirmy sort of feeling in my tummy. I knew this was nothing to do with my own situation and that this in some way related to her. After quite a long silence, when she still seemed quite unable to speak, I asked, 'I'm wondering if you perhaps have a kind of squirmy feeling inside?' At this I got a real response. She looked at me directly, with astonishment, and nodded. I said, 'Something pretty scary must have happened.' Again she nodded, holding my gaze. 'Can you tell me about it?' I asked. 'It might help to share it. Was it one of the topics I mentioned?' Another nod. I said that I guessed one of the most difficult to talk about might be being raped; was it this? This time she began to talk and told me about a most horrific incident of rape by a former boyfriend. It had been a deliberate and vicious attack but in her own home, which she had allowed him to enter. Because of this she perceived it to be her fault and was loath to tell the police about it. In fact, in time she did. The woman police specialist who had dealt with rape victims for some twenty years said it was the worst rape case that she had ever dealt with, causing a lot of internal damage to the girl.

The work of therapy continued but the point of this extract is to see how we can arrive at the focus of the sessions. In this example it was achieved by using silence, countertransference/projective identification, education, questions, noticing the body language and picking up on the weight of feeling in the room, and providing a sufficiently safe environment for the client to open up. This demonstrates the flexibility of the therapist.

Body memory

Another technique that is extremely valuable I call the body memory exercise, and it is one that can speed up the process very much. An example of this used in practice follows, and an example of how to lead this is shown in the quick reference notes at the end of the chapter. It is especially useful when a client is depressed but has absolutely no idea why. Once we have explored the obvious, already mentioned things with them, such as anniversaries, key life events, and so on, I will then suggest that we try an exercise and I explain how it works. It was used with the following client.

Rob

Rob was terrified of going into lectures and was in danger of dropping out of the course. He had no idea why, but simply found himself unable to go into the lecture hall.

Having explored various ideas and drawn a blank I asked, 'When you think about going into the lecture theatre, what happens in your body? Do you experience any tension?' He wasn't sure. I suggested that we might try an exercise to see, explaining that sometimes the body will remember a trauma that the conscious mind has forgotten. If we can get in touch with the body memory we can, sometimes, bring the trauma into the consciousness so that it can be dealt with. Rob was happy to try. So I asked him to shut his eyes, relax and then to think about going to the lecture theatre, to visualize himself walking towards it and to be very conscious of what was happening in his body as he did this. He felt a tension across the palms of both his hands. I asked him to be very aware of this tension and concentrate on it and then to imagine himself getting smaller and smaller and to see if an image or person or situation came to mind. I asked him to indicate with his hand if he did have a mental picture but to stay with the picture. This was all said in a quiet and gentle tone, so as not to intrude into the situation. In fact he did have a memory, so I asked him to tell me about it. 'Where are you?' He was in Africa. 'How old are you? What are you wearing?'

I deliberately use the present tense as I ask these questions so that it pushes the client further into the memory and the reliving of that memory. In the memory, he was a little boy of about five and he was standing in front of his uncle, who was beating him across the palms of his hand with a stick. This was in front of a large number of people. He had been asked to run and fetch the milk from the other side of the forest and had been too terrified to do so, so had not obeyed. He felt utterly humiliated to be shown up in front of all these people. I asked what the little boy wanted to say to the uncle. He couldn't say, so I asked him to go into the scene as his adult self and to stand with the little boy and speak for him.

'What do you want to say to the uncle?'

'Leave him alone. He's much too small to have been asked to go to the other side of the forest on his own. Don't you realize he's never done that before? And it's not fair to chastise him in front of everyone. You're a bully!'

I asked, 'What do you want to do with the little boy?'

'I want to take him in my arms and comfort him, but that would shame him, too. So I'd take him by the hand and say to the uncle, "I'll go with him across the forest and fetch what is needed. Now go and fight someone your own size." Out of sight of the others, I would want to hold the little one in my arms and comfort him and tell him it's all right and all right to be frightened, because he would have got lost and that it was not fair of the uncle.'

I then asked Rob, when he was ready, to come back to the counselling room, bringing the little boy if he wished, so that we could look at what had happened. He did so, surprised at the memory. He had forgotten all about that incident.

Together then we explored how this episode could relate to the lectures. He found it easy to make the link. The crowds! The people! Being asked to speak in front of them all! It being a, sort of, school-like situation, a learning one, as it had been at five, with someone in charge, the lecturer, like his uncle. Since he was African, in a strange place, where he still didn't know his way around and sometimes not even the language very well, this linked, too. And so we had discovered the focal area and he had re-experienced the painful emotions of the time and to some degree put the situation right in retrospect.

He was still, however, left with the residue of the panic with regard to the lecture hall, since this now was a habit. We needed to address that too. I tackled that in two ways. First, I taught him a very simple relaxation exercise that he could do several times a day and could also do especially when approaching the lecture hall, or any crowded situation. The more practised he could become at this the quicker the actual exercise could work to help him. It is a very simple exercise of clenching and relaxing the muscles bit by bit all over the body. Eventually, just by clenching a hand, the body should go into relaxation mode.

The second thing that I suggested he do was to take the little boy by the hand as he approached any of these scary situations. Then, he had to consciously remind the little one, in his imagination, that he, the adult, was with him now and that he could answer back and speak up for the two of them. The situation, therefore, was not as it had been in front of his uncle. I wondered if there had been a pet name that he might have been called as a little boy, because that could help in this exercise. In fact, Bobby was the child's pet name. I further suggested that he could perhaps devise a short-cut code to remind himself that he was not in the forest and that he's not five but thirty-five. This is to help keep him in the present and not get hooked into the past. For example, he might simply have to say, 'It's OK Bobby, Robert's here' or 'I'm Robert' or 'Bobby, you go and play – I'll see to this', or whatever helps!

So he had a lot of 'homework' to do. When he next came to see me he had begun to go to classes and felt very much better. The progress continued. After just three sessions he felt that he had no further need of therapy. He was now fine, not only attending classes but even speaking in a hall about some political issue to some three hundred people! I was delighted, of course, if a bit surprised. I asked what had helped, expecting some reference at least to the body exercise that we had done, which seemed to me to be a vital component and on which I had been congratulating myself! This, however, got no mention at all. He said it was the relaxation exercise that had done the trick. He had practised this thirty and forty times a day. When I prodded a little (hopefully!?) for what else might have helped he said, 'God!' 'Well, that put me in my place!' I thought. I could not deny that one, but persisted, and asked if the work around the uncle had also helped. He thought that perhaps it had. I believe it had played a major part in the remarkable shift, but readers will have to make up their own minds. The body work here was combined with a gestalt exercise. Once we had actually pinpointed the painful memory, we moved straight into that while the moment was right.

Again, in this example there are a number of skills employed by the therapist and it demonstrates the flexibility required, to maintain the energy and pace of the work. By changing what is happening in the picture that emerges from the body memory the issues also alter.

Fantasy exercise

The same can happen with a fantasy exercise, such as in the example below. Although the therapist asks a question that leads the client into such a fantasy exercise it is very much in the hands of the client as to where they go with it. It is the therapist's job to support and ensure that the client ends in a safe place with it.

Client E

In Rawson, 2002, pp. 97–99, there is an example of me relying very much on where the client led. Although I was with her in her fantasy journey, I had absolutely no idea what was coming next. I endeavoured, at each stage, to help her to make it safe or possible, but she was the one who worked out how, mostly to my total amazement. An extract below, in which 'P' stands for me and 'E' for the client, demonstrates what I mean. I was aware of time being short and wanted to bring E out of the fantasy and back to the room. She had created a horse as a symbol of safety for herself and they were out: 'in a plain . . . it's green and there's lots of space.'

> P: 'Can you get to the College, to the classroom. Will the horse bring you?'
> E: 'Yes, he's here – I've opened a window and his head's poking in.'
> P: 'That's not very practical – can he change again to be closer?'
> E: 'Yes he's changing shape, he's a dragon draped around my shoulders.'
> P: 'Can he get smaller; he'll frighten the others.'
> E: 'Yes, he's quite small now – under my collar – like a necklace around my neck – comforting.'
> P: 'Has he a name?'
> E: 'Yes – Horace. That came up this morning.' (and she told me of an incident that morning.)
> P: 'So how do you feel about what we've been doing today?'
> E: 'Good – it feels like integration. I don't think I'll lose this – it's easier to hold on to images.'

As you can see, I'm being very matter of fact, observing the problem of size but leaving her to work out how to solve it, which she does: 'Yes, he's changing shape . . .'

So the moral here is to be alert, go with the client, help them to make it safe and to move it along, but trust the client to have the answers. It is their trip, we are just facilitating, but by our presence we are both 'catalysts' and 'safety nets'. But as observers, outside the emotional entanglements, we can make suggestions in order to make it safe. You recall that with Rob I encouraged him to bring his adult self in to speak up for little Bobby. Had he found that difficult, I might have brought myself into the picture saying something like: 'Well, I'd like to take the child by the hand and say to uncle . . .'

Really one has to react at the time to the situation that is presented. One reacts with common sense and compassion combined with whatever skills one has at one's disposal.

Practice and supervision

If you are not familiar with this type of work I suggest that you can try this exercise on your own, or with a colleague, or perhaps in your supervision, until you feel comfortable enough with it to try it with clients.

Homework

As mentioned previously, I give the clients 'homework'. In this way they can progress the work during the week. I return to it here as one would in the therapy, session by session. If the client does not do the homework, that too can be part of the learning process. Why haven't they? What were the obstacles? If it is not done, it is not the role of the therapist to be in any way punitive. It may well be that the work suggested was way off the mark from where the client was. It is something to explore with the client.

Activity

The flexibility required of the therapist in this method also points to an activity of the therapist which is unfamiliar to some. Chapter Seven addresses this.

QUICK REFERENCE NOTES

Body memory exercise

Before using the body memory exercise with the client

The client needs to be aware of the rationale behind this exercise and to agree to give it a try. So one explains to the client that the body remembers even things that, with our conscious minds, we do not, and that using a body memory exercise we can sometimes get in touch with such memories. Then these memories can be dealt with appropriately, so that they no longer inhibit our freedom in the present time. It helps to give the cliient an example as to how this can work; for instance, as with Rob, who was cited earlier. Then see if the client would like to try this method.

A great deal can emerge in this exercise

Therapists new to this exercise are often astounded at how much can emerge from it. The memories that come up often move the therapy along very quickly; at times, it can be very emotional and powerful. Sufficient time needs to be allowed for it within the session so that the client ends in a good place. If the exercise is begun near the start of the session there should be time enough to do the exercise and to talk about the material that has come up before the end of the session. I suggest that ten minutes is allowed for the client to say where they are since the last session and to settle into the therapeutic work once more, and then twenty minutes for the exercise and twenty minutes to talk about it afterwards.

Creativity required of the therapist

The therapist needs to be able to work with the client to

move the emerging scenes on. In using this method one needs to be very creative and work with where the client is, but remember the client can be creative, too. Sometimes one wonders where the scene is going and what to do with it, but one can say things like, 'Can you find a way of dealing with that?' Invariably the client can and does.

A safe place

One needs to help the client to reach a safe place with their story. I have referred to E above, and the full example appears in Rawson, 2002, pp. 97–99. This is is an example of me relying very much on where the client led. Although I was with her in her fantasy journey, I had absolutely no idea what was coming next. I endeavoured, at each stage, to help her to make it safe or possible, but she was the one who worked out how, mostly to my total amazement. I was aware of time being short and wanted to bring the client out of the fantasy and back to the room. She had created a horse as a symbol of safety for herself and through her imagination, she was able to transform this into a manageable symbol of a necklace.

How to begin

After the explanation about what the exercise is, it may begin as follows:

'If you'd like to close your eyes so that you do not get distracted and just breathe normally. Be aware of any tension anywhere in your body. Indicate in some way if you have found any tension, raise a hand or finger perhaps. (Wait until the client has responded – a minute or two.) Be very aware of the tension and make the tension worse. See if it moves. If it does move, follow it to where it is now, be very aware of it and make it worse. See if it stays put or if it moves again. If it moves, follow it, be aware of it, make it worse. Continue to do this until it remains in one place and indicate when it has settled in the one place.' (If the client seems stuck you can encourage by repeating the words: be very aware of the tension and when it stops in one place just indicate so that I know you're there.)

'Good. Now concentrate again on the tension. Be very aware of it. Let your mind float free, with you getting smaller and smaller and see what pops into your mind, no matter how irrelevant it seems. Try to catch that thought, or picture, or thing, and if you have one indicate in some way so that I know.

'Can you share it with me?'

If the client is clearly staying within the scene in their minds, e.g., having their eyes still closed as they answer this, the therapist may continue straight on with the exercise, leading the client into the scene as follows.

The therapist helps the client to fill in the detail in the scene. 'What is happening? . . . How old are you? . . . Who else is there?'. . . or, if the client opens their eyes and clearly is back in the present talking about the situation that they have seen, then the therapist will adopt more of a discursive tone to find out what was going on in the fantasy and might speak thus: 'Did a memory or picture or situation come to mind?'.

Some clients do have a memory, some do not. If not, it is not important. Now that they have run through the technique, it is one that they can try on their own. On their own, they may feel more free and less inhibited and can share what emerges at the next session.

Sometimes what comes up can be very dramatic, eliciting tears, or anger, or shock. At times it is something quite ordinary, and often it is something that they had completely forgotten about.

Bringing the client back to the room

(If the client is slow to open their eyes, repeat: 'When you are ready come back to the room and open your eyes so that I know that you are ready' . . . or later: 'Even if you have no image or picture slowly come back to the room and open your eyes' . . .)

Time running out

If the client is not ready when the time is running out the therapist can say something along the lines of: 'If you're not quite finished with your scene, either finish off now or tell everyone there that you have to go now but you'll be back later, and then gently return to the room and open your eyes' . . . and a little later, if needed, I'll chivvy a bit more: 'Come back to the room now, please, so find a safe place for all in the scene and come back to the room and open your eyes.'

From the recent memory repeat the exercise to find an earlier picture

Sometimes it is a very recent memory or event that they picture and they cannot see why it should be a cause of the tension. This often happens. What one needs to do then is to repeat the exercise using this memory as the starting point and see if an earlier memory comes up. Often there are links to be found, at a later point, between the last and the earlier scenes. The term 'smaller and smaller' is used rather than 'younger and younger' because it is less specific.

I explain that we are going to once again get in touch with the tension, starting with the picture that has already emerged and seeing if we can access the earliest memory that is linked with that tension. We will do this by being aware of the tension once more: 'Visualise that situation as clearly as you can and then see if you have any tension in your body.' Again the tension will be followed around the body until it settles in one place and then: 'Let your mind float free, then capture any image that comes, no matter how seemingly irrelevant'. The therapist then helps the client to go into the scene and to fill in as much detail as possible. We encourage the client to give the people voices and actions: what do they want to say, first one then another, what do they reply, what do they do? Do they want to take someone else into the scene, e.g., the tutor or therapist, an older self, or some other trusted person who can be 'on their side'? What do they want that person to do or say? At times, if it seems necessary, I'll put myself as therapist into the scene and ease the situation that is emerging there. This can help the client to move on within the scene. To facilitate the client developing the scene that has come up for them, the therapist asks questions such as ' Where are you?' . . . 'What are you doing?' . . . 'What is the place like?' . . . 'What are you wearing?' . . . 'Who else is there?' . . . 'How old are you?' This time, the therapist helps the client to get the people in the scene talking to each other. The therapist asks questions such as: 'What do they want to say?' . . . 'What do they reply?' . . . 'What do they do?' . . . 'Do you want to take some-one else into the scene, perhaps a tutor or therapist, or your older self, or some other trusted person who can be on your side?' . . . 'What do you want that person to do or say?' . . . As the client shares what they are picturing at each stage, the therapist needs to go with the flow, adapting their questions to help move the scene along and to help the client to benefit from the experience.

Sometimes the client remains fairly silent, alone with their scene. One can discuss with them, once they have an idea as to how the exercise goes, whether they want to share at each stage or to be allowed simply to go into the picture on their own and then to share. The fact that the therapist is there is enough to provide the feeling of safety for the client. The exercise might then proceed along the following lines:

'Close your eyes to block out the room and become aware of the tension in your body, chase it round as before until it stops. Then let your mind go free and see if a picture or image or scene pops into your mind no matter how irrelevant and catch it. Please indicate when you have found one. Now you have a few minutes to go into the scene as I suggested before, see what happens and when you're ready come back to the room slowly and open your eyes so that I know you are back.' I then allow a few minutes. If there seems an overly long delay I gently say something as shown above along the lines of: 'If you're not quite finished with your scene, either finish off now or put it on hold until later and then gently come back to the room and open your eyes' and a little later, if needed, I'll chivvy a bit more: 'You need to finish now, please, and open your eyes.'

The client and therapist would then explore together what came up in the exercise.

Tone of voice

The tone of voice used when leading the client into this exercise needs to be very quiet and gentle, almost soporific, as one tries to lead as unobtrusively as possible.

Flexibility re skills used by the therapist

In focal and brief therapy, the range of skills and the flexibility of the therapist in applying these is paramount. This type of therapy requires *activity* on the part of the therapist.

Examples of range of skills

- Use of all usual therapy techniques blended to challenge/coax/hold/ the client as required.
- Use of the therapeutic relationship.
- Use of Rogerian approach, e.g., unconditional positive regard.
- Use of transference – working with it and within it.
- Use of some aspects of behavioural work.
- Use of psychodynamic principles – past influencing the present.
- Skills to access the past – body work/gestalt/fantasy/ use of voice (almost hypnotic), intellectual research also (homework for the client sheet).
- Use of art/music/writing/ imagery.
- Focusing techniques – selective inattention.
- Skills with tone of voice, body language, silence.

CHAPTER SEVEN

ACTIVITY

This approach to therapy is active. It is not just the therapist who is active but also the client. The client doing 'homework', or work between sessions on their own is one aspect of this. This has already been touched upon. It is a very important way in which the therapy is speeded up. On average, the client, one must remember, sees the therapist for just an hour per week. If clients can be helped to work on their issues between sessions, progress will be quicker.

Working with the client/homework/ giving them the tools

The joint aspect of the therapy work is emphasized in their working on the issues between sessions. This homework may take the form of a specific exercise, or it may be suggested that the client seek out relevant people in their past lives to talk to, or they might decide to research a particular time in their lives. The homework might be to be aware of a particular emotion that occurs as they go about their day to day activities and to monitor it. This, initially, is just to heighten awareness. Later on, the client and therapist may discuss and look for alternative ways that the client might respond that might change a situation for the better. More will be said about this idea later.

The important thing with regard to the homework is that it arises out of the session and that it takes the work forward.

In the following example we can see how useful some homework can be. Again, this is combined with some 'education'. People are often very unaware of the psychological and emotional impact of situations and they need to be taught about them, so that they are empowered to become their own therapists.

Jane

Jane was very upset about how her child reacted when she went out for the evening. Her child became very upset every time she went out. I asked what happened. It turned out that the child wanted to know where her mother – a single parent in her late twenties – was going and when she would be back. This, for Jane, had echoes of her teens and early twenties when her own mother had questioned her in this way. She was reacting to her child, Holly, as if it were her mother talking. So she refused to tell her. I asked how old was her child. Holly was seven. I said that it seemed quite reasonable to me that a child should be able to access her mother when she went out, and that, maybe, the babysitter could be given the number so that, if there was a problem, the child could make contact. I wondered whether perhaps she was forgetting that she was the mother and Holly just a child. A child who was dependent upon her and therefore felt lost, abandoned, and threatened when she was just left with the babysitter and, especially, because of Jane's refusal to tell her anything, she was frightened. None of this had occurred to Jane, she was so deeply into the transference. I suggested that she might give it a try. I asked how old she felt when this happened? She began to realize that she was indeed projecting feelings from her teenage years on to her little daughter. She could see that they really related to the unfinished business with her mother. We explored that further, but she also tried giving more information to the babysitter and she let her daughter know that the babysitter had the contact numbers.

When she returned for her next session the situation was quite different. She had devised a card system for her daughter and she had written all the numbers where she could be contacted if necessary, and the babysitter knew of this. Additionally, she gave her daughter a special treat and time for the two of them to be together on another day in the week, to emphasize that she loved being with her, too, but also needed time with adult friends as well and hence her nights out. The daughter now had no problem letting her go and no longer caused any fuss at all.

In this instance, she both did the homework and more than we had agreed together. She had made it her own.

Parent–adult–child interactions

Another useful way of looking at relationships and at the interactions between people, is the idea often associated with transactional analysis (TA). As for the Heimler Social Functioning scale referred to earlier, one can undertake a three-year course in this method. Once again, the basic concept can be very useful and clients can readily learn to monitor their relationships using it. Essentially, we all tend to relate to each other as parent, adult, and child. We take up different roles, at different times. We may be parent–parent, or child–child, or adult–adult. We are, at times, child–parent, or adult–parent, or child–adult. In the example of Jane, above, we saw her in an inappropriate role with her child, Holly. Jane was acting the child and putting her seven-year-old daughter Holly in the parent role. That is, until she realized what was happening. Then she retrieved her parent role in relation to her daughter, her adult role in going out for some adult company and relaxation, and her internal child was back in place once more. This instead of being the rebellious teenager, determined to have a night out whatever her 'mother' thought. It might be that, in the having fun out with her mates, the inner child could also have appropriately surfaced once more.

This theory is often depicted as two triangles, each representing a person, with each point representing either parent, adult, or child. The interactions can then be drawn out between the two triangles. A couple can learn to monitor their moves between the roles. It is clearly not desirable if both are permanently in child mode, or even parent mode. Equally, it is not so good if one is always the parent and one always the child. There are, of course, times when two adults might both be in adult–parent role, for example, as they decide their children's schooling, or chores around the house, or discipline, or child role as they have fun together. If one partner is upset, the other may take on a temporary parent role, at another time the other partner may assume that role. It is a matter of common sense and balance and such a concept is easily grasped by the clients. They can then keep a watchful eye on their own relationships, and in seeing, begin to effect change if it is needed.

Non compliance with homework

If a client does not do the homework it is important not to be punitive. They may have moved on and our suggestion is irrelevant. We may be too far away in our suggestion from their real issue, they may simply not have had time, or perhaps it is altogether too scary to undertake on their own. Sometimes this can be the case, and they prefer to undertake the homework task in the counselling room, with us there, or simply to talk about the particular thing they had intended to do. It needs to be a task that they can see to be useful. It may be relevant to query why it was not done, but they are adults and if it is not helpful then that is fine. The sessions are for their benefit, and the therapist is merely the facilitator, so needs to work harder to find what is helpful. However, it might also indicate a certain lack of rapport, or a mismatch with regard to the contract – have we contracted to look at what they really want to work on? Or there may be a disparity with regard to expectations as to how therapy can work, or a lack of commitment to the therapy. Some clients expect the therapist to wave a magic wand and all their problems will be resolved; that is not what happens. Our role is to facilitate their journey. We can use all our skills to help but, ultimately, it is their trip. It may be that they simply want to come along for some support and do not want to change anything. This can happen.

I recall Janina, who was in a relationship with four different men simultaneously. She was finding this very problematic and exhausting, as she juggled her life to keep each part of it secret from the other. She had absolutely no intention of rationalizing her situation, but she did want to share with me her difficulties in running her life like this. This was not a contract I could see as feasible, since she simply wanted to have a periodic moan. Had she wanted to change anything in her situation, or to explore why she was choosing to live in this way, we could have proceeded. As it was, there was no place for brief therapy.

Situations that cannot be changed

There are times when support is all that *is* possible. There are situations that cannot be changed, such as when someone is a carer, or in an impossible job, and unable to change it. In these circumstances I would see it as perfectly appropriate for a therapist to be there for the client, but this would not be a brief therapy contract. Such circumstances could go on for some time, even years. It might become a brief contract, or series of brief contracts, by the person coming periodically for a few sessions to see the therapist in order to look at particular aspects of their circumstances and to explore options or attitudes to these. The important angle here is that both client and therapist are in agreement as to what they are about and that the therapist is in a position to offer what is required.

Client F

Another example of the value of homework can be found in Rawson, 2002, p. 77, in the case of F, who has already been mentioned in passing in this book. This client had had no faith whatsoever in the idea of therapy and had turned up for the appointment just to please the nurse who had sent her. Her opening words had given me the clue to her issue: 'I've been depressed since I was nine'. I explained to her how therapy works, how the root to the problem is often in the past, and if not dealt with can cause us ongoing problems, including 'depression'. I told her the sorts of issues that might have occurred to cause a problem, including bullying at school, moving home and changing schools or jobs if relevant, illness in the family, a death, break-up of relationship, or change of circumstance of some kind or another. F was utterly sceptical and totally unconvinced. I wagered that she would discover that something of significance had occurred and that it had affected her around the age of nine. She remained sceptical and doubtful. I strongly challenged her to see for herself and to try to find out. Her homework was to 'create a chronology of events from as far back as she could remember, and to help her with this I suggested that she might ask members of her family and friends about what had happened in the family, especially when she was nine. I asked her to let me know how it went in the next session. I left her free to do it or not, as she chose, but requested that she let me know if she did not intend to keep her appointment. I also told her that if she did not find anything significant, I still believed that I could help her with this long term 'depression' and we could continue to explore the situation. In fact, before her next session, I received a long letter from her in which she had indeed discovered that enormous things were going on for the family around when she was nine. F was now a convert to the idea of therapy and looking forward to her session to explore it all further!

Homework to alter patterns of behaviour

A client who reacts in a particular, but undesirable, way in certain circumstances can be given homework to begin the process towards altering the pattern of the unwanted behaviour. For example, in the first instance, they can be asked simply to note the behaviour. This is the first step to awareness. The next stage might be to see what were the circumstances leading to this behaviour or reaction. Catching themselves in the middle of the reaction or just afterwards they might ask themselves: 'How old do I feel?'; 'What am I feeling right now?'; 'What do I want to do in this situation?'; 'Who does this person remind me of?' They can then explore some of these situations with the therapist at the next session. As we explore with the client what was happening when they were ten, or twenty, or whatever age they have discovered, so we are into the psychodynamic aspect of brief therapy. Equally, we see the psychodynamic aspect as the client realizes that they feel murderous, at times, towards their boss because they see him as their dad, who was equally unreasonable with them as a child. It is their transference that they are discovering and with which we are to work. Then, with greater understanding, as they continue to observe the instances of the unwanted behaviour, they can begin to change it. They can rehearse a different way of responding. For example, if x always provokes an angry response when they do y, now the client, with their greater understanding, might change the angry retort into the real emotion they have become aware of, such as: 'I feel hurt when you do or say that'. This, in itself, will change the pattern of what has been happening.

An aspect of transference

The question: 'How old do you feel?', or, if you are a therapist practising the exercise on yourself: 'How old do I feel?', can often bring up all sorts of memories that may be colouring the present for us. People transfer their reactions and feeling on to a present situation. These behaviours, however, are often inappropriate to the present. The past and present need to be disentangled, so that the person is free to behave appropriately in the present.

Frasier

There was a good example of transference in a *Frasier* programme from the television series. Frasier is going out with a PE teacher, who derides a girl who is rather bad at PE and holds the class back until this child has climbed the ropes. This reminds Frasier, who observes the incident, of himself at school, when he was the one who couldn't do the PE task. He and the viewer immediately see his current girlfriend as if she was the old male teacher, who can only be described as rather grizzly-looking and very hairy. Having this picture in his mind rather cools his relationship with his girlfriend; that is, until he eventually challenges her about her rough handling of the less able pupil. In doing this, he is making a challenge he had been unable to make as a child and so freeing himself of the entanglement of his transference. His girlfriend accepts his comments and the situation is resolved. The viewer once again sees the pretty girlfriend on the screen as opposed to the rather less than pretty male PE teacher of Frasier's youth. All is well until he makes a comment like

'That little girl reminded me of myself at that age in PE.' Immediately, his girlfriend imagines Frasier in a gym slip and with pigtails, like the little girl she had been castigating for being inept. The viewer now sees Frasier as the little girl, incongruously talking authoritatively about the table reservations at the posh restaurant that Frasier and his lady friend were going to. Her transference is now what we are seeing and clearly is blocking the relationship once again. Their story ends there. The aim of therapy is that the client is helped first to become aware of their transference and then to deal with it, as Frasier did.

Short term, active, flexible, *and* psychodynamic

I highlight the above instance to stress the psychodynamic nature of the brief approach. Although it is brief, it is deep and does deal with past issues. It is not a sticking plaster approach. It does not require forever to access the past. It is, perhaps, the activity of both therapist and client that helps to access the past quickly.

Some students attending my courses have seen the approach as more integrative than psychodynamic because they have a different concept of psychodynamic, one that would even recommend that the therapist should sit on her/his hands rather than gesticulate. I was astonished at this idea. Where lies the idea of congruence in it, I wonder? I recall the story of a man who had been so advised and found himself totally unable to articulate without using his hands. I fully support the views of Wolberg, who states that the activity required of 'the aspiring short-term therapist' assumes 'an involvement of oneself as a real person, and open expression of interest, sympathy and encouragement, are permissible' (Wolberg, 1965, p. 135). As I observe 'This is in stark contrast to the stoical and expressionless passivity that somehow has become "synonymous with doing good psychotherapy"' (Rawson, 2002, p. 113). Other early proponents echo this, too. Malan, for example, observes that the face to face method of therapy 'encourages interaction and activity' (*ibid.*)

For those who wish to look more at the psychodynamic roots of the approach I would refer you to Rawson, 2002, pp. 68–82.

Fusion of skills and still psychodynamic

The therapist is active in many ways: actively questioning, using techniques and skills from a range of disciplines. The method allows a 'fusion' of skills, as we have already seen when we explored the flexibility of the therapist in this approach. While I like the word 'fusion' here, I do not see it as so different from the word integrative. The important thing is that one can combine skills, as Wolberg suggests, but stay firmly within the psychodynamic tradition. You will recall that the early proponents of the brief approach in the 1940s and 1960s, who were mostly analysts by profession, also recommended this flexibility of skills (Rawson, 2002, pp. 82–110). We noted earlier this flexibility in looking at the experienced therapist, who has access to more skills simply because they've been around in the therapy world longer. The experienced therapist may dare to step out of the rigidity of their original training to take on board the value of other approaches.

Having stressed activity, it must be pointed out that this does not preclude silence. At times maybe as much as twenty minutes might pass without a word being spoken. An example of this was quoted earlier when I worked with sixteen-year-old Jacques.

Having talked a lot about activity and the use of a range of skills, it is time to actually look at some of these in the next chapter. These might be employed by the therapist to speed the work along. The wider the therapist's experience and skills, the more able they are to adapt to the client's need.

QUICK REFERENCE NOTES

Activity

- Activity of therapist
  - by holding the focus, keeping the 'spotlight' on the agreed focus;
  - by holding boundaries;
  - by actively holding a silence;
  - by facilitating, e.g., use of questions, use of art, fantasy exercises, body memory exercise, use of transference, countertransference;
  - by being in 'sprint mode', sensitively aware of inflections, body movements, hesitations, actively holding client to agreed contract;
  - by being flexible re techniques and contract, moving with client to a new contracted focus/time scale as necessary;
  - by explaining the processes of counselling and how various techniques might be helpful, i.e., teaching the client how to be their own therapist;
  - by giving information, e.g., psychological process of grief;
  - by being actively involved while remaining appropriately detached;
  - by researching subjects as necessary.

Working with the client – giving them the tools: homework

A joint enterprise

For example,

> 'You're the one who needs to be doing the work.'
>
> 'You can speed the process up by doing some working between sessions.'
>
> 'We need to be a little like detectives – exploring together – we need to look in detail at . . .'

Tools for clients to become own therapist

> 'The next time you experience the feeling take note of the events preceding it and what had just happened. Where were you? What were you doing, etc? – then we can talk about it next session.'
>
> 'The next time you are in that situation see how old you feel and we'll talk about it in the next session. Write the whole incident down if it helps.'
>
> 'The next time you feel that emotion note where the tension is in your body and do the body memory exercise we've used together and see what comes up.'

Other 'homework' to move therapy on

> 'Check your diaries to see if these dates are important.'
>
> 'Can you talk to any of your relatives about what was happening at that time in your childhood?'
>
> 'Try to be aware of when you do *x*' (whatever the client is trying to change).
>
> 'Plan how you'd like to change this and try it!'
>
> 'Reward yourself each time you notice the behaviour, manage to modify it or change it.'

'Record your dreams.'

'Write about the key events of your life.'

'Paint/draw the emotion.'

'Write a poem/letter to the person you miss/love/hate – not to send.'

'Write down the feelings and thoughts you have as openly as possible – bring them to the session or burn them.'

'Decide on a course of action and take at least one step to achieve it, e.g., enrolling at an evening class, attending the next lecture.'

'Act out a symbolic ritual, e.g., light a candle as a meaningful way of remembering/making amends/saying goodbye.'

'Think about which of the areas you've mentioned you want to explore – and that's where we'll begin next time.'

'Talk to the child – see what he/she has to say.'

'Use the relaxation exercise every time you feel tense.'

'See whether you are behaving as parent–adult or child in the relationship – in what role is the other person?'

BE YOUR OWN THERAPIST!

CHAPTER EIGHT

TECHNIQUES

The following techniques call upon different skills and demand activity either on the part of both client or therapist or on the part of the client.

Working with body tension

One way of working with body tension has been shown earlier, both within the text in case examples and in the quick reference notes as an outline of a body memory exercise. Tension in the body is often present because of some stress or another. Often it is not clear as to what is causing the tension. There are other ways to work with this symptom of stress. One of these ways is as follows.

I ask the client, 'Would you like to try a fantasy exercise to see if we can do anything with the tension?' Assuming a yes answer, I would then say, 'Feel free to stop at any time or to ask questions.'

'Close your eyes to cut out the distractions in the room.

'Now become very conscious of the tension in your body . . .

'Tell me about it/more about it . . . Has it got a colour? . . . What shape is it? . . . What texture?' . . .

It is then up to the therapist to help the client work creatively with this. Examples of directions you might give are:

'Can you make it smaller/bigger/ make a hole in it, take it out and discard it/transform it? . . . Can you bring light into it? . . . Can you bring in anyone else to help? . . . You can bring me in if you like . . . What do you want them/me to do? . . . What is happening now? . . . Can you change that to make it safer/ok/easier/lighter/etc?' . . .

When you feel it is the right moment to end the exercise, either because it has reached a good point or because the time is running out, make comments like:

'That seems a really good place to end, so can you leave it there/bring that with you/file that away for a look at later, or file it in the archives or in the bin/find a way to leave comfortably what you have been doing and come back to the room and open your eyes.'

The client may well come up with a surprising way to end.

Client and therapist then discuss what has happened, and what can be learned from the exercise and any follow-up that makes sense in relation to it. Always allow at least ten minutes for this part of the exercise. I would suggest, ideally, to aim to end the fantasy twenty minutes before the end of the session.

A rough guide might be to see the session in three blocks of twenty minutes – the first seeing where the client is and deciding to try this technique, twenty minutes for the fantasy activity, and then the review and decision for future action.

Fantasy exercise using body tension and imagery

There is another type of fantasy exercise that could be used working with body tension. This is similar to the above but using different imagery. The first part of the exercise would be the same as above.

I ask the client, 'Would you like to try a fantasy exercise to see if we can do anything with the tension?' Assuming a yes answer, I would say, 'Feel free to stop at any time or to ask questions.' Then

'Close your eyes to cut out the distractions in the room.

'Now become very conscious of the tension in your body.

'Can you name an animal/bird that depicts the feeling?

'What is it like?

'What are its qualities?

'Can you let it leave your body?

'Where is it now?

'What do you want to do with it?

'Do you need anyone or anything to help you with it? If so bring whatever helps into the situation . . .

'When you have achieved what you wanted to, come back to the room and open your eyes.'

The first question I would want to ask is, 'What has happened to the tension that was in your body?'

I would expect a considerable change in the feeling, and often quite a lot of thoughtfulness, subsequent to the fantasy exercise. At times, the client has new insight into what might be causing their tension. At other times, they find that what came up is intriguing but cannot relate it to their situation. In this case, we explore possibilities and I ask them to fill me in on what has gone on, if that has not been happening stage by stage through the exercise.

It is perhaps better to ask the client at each stage what is happening, so that one can adapt and go with the flow as to the next question. In this, one needs to be creative, use common sense and seek for a safe place to end. If a neat ending is not possible in the time available, then, at least, one seeks for a safe holding place. The client is usually well able to find one.

Fantasy for a relationship difficulty

This animal/plant/object fantasy could be used differently, for example, if the client was having difficulty in a relationship or with a boss. They could be asked to 'Visualize the other person as an animal/plant/bird or object' without any reference to body tension. The rest of the exercise could continue as follows.

'What qualities does the chosen creature have?

'How does it make you feel?

'What animal /plant/bird do you see yourself as?

'What qualities do you have?

'How does it respond to you?

'How do you respond to the other creature?

'What do you want to do?

'What does it tell you about yourself in the situation?

'Can you change yourself into a different animal/plant/ object so that you can cope better or enjoy the situation more?

'Can you bring anyone else into the situation to help?

'Can you find a positive way to complete the story, or

to safely put it in abeyance and return to the room? If you are in difficulty with this let me know so that I can help.'

Talking to the block

In a similar way, if someone finds themselves stuck or blocked from doing something, and not knowing what it is about, they might try talking to it. Authors often talk of writers' block and this exercise could be useful. I recall a student, Geoff, who was totally unable to get on with the assigned essay. Normally he was well able to do his work so this was unusual. When I asked the subject matter, it was about alcoholism. The obvious question seemed to be whether he knew of anyone in his family or close circle who was alcoholic. It transpired that there was indeed. His mother had recently been hopitalized for this problem. Once he had made the connection to his own personal life he was well able to separate the two and deal appropriately with the essay. It is not always that easy. In other cases of such a block one could try to engage the block in conversation, adapting the questions above or combining with one of the visualizing exercises above. For example, one could give the block a shape or colour as a starting point. I recall Anthony, who was finding that his knees were bothering him to the extent that he was unable to walk. He talked to them and it emerged that he really had no inclination to go to where he was due to go. Once he had put his finger on the real issue he found that the knees were no longer so painful and in fact he was able once more to move more or less freely.

Talking to the inner child

At times, the client is well aware that they are responding to a situation as if they were a child. They feel about twelve, for example. They can be encouraged to imagine themselves at twelve and to have a conversation with their inner child.

Kate

'Can you remember an instance when you were that age?'
   'Where are you?'
   'What was happening?'
   'What were you wearing?'
   'Did you have a pet name as a child? For example, Kitty?'
   'Talk to little Kitty. What does she want to say to you?'
   'What do you want to say?'
   'What does she reply?'
These exercises can be very powerful and very revealing. They can move the client along very quickly. Not all clients find it easy to do this. That is all right. Try something else! It may, however, still be worth explaining the exercise to the client, in case they wish to try it on their own at home. Some find this useful and easier to do alone rather than with the therapist present. For those who fear the powerfulness of the exercise and wonder if what emerges can be contained, one must remember that the client has been 'containing' whatever it is for many years and is basically in charge. Whatever was so terrifying or awful that it was buried by the child may not be that terrible for the adult who now looks at it.

Fantasy exercises

The fantasy exercises I referred to above can be very effective as we saw in case example E, earlier, which is cited in more detail in Rawson, 2002, pp. 95–99. I do not know why the fantasy work works, I just see examples in my practice where it does. It seems that the client can change their reality by changing the fantasy. Does working with the fantasy perhaps make it more safe for the client, does it tune in to the unconscious and allow those forces to be altered so that it also alters the conscious? Does it in some way consciously reprogramme a habitual maladaptive pattern lying deep in the unconscious? When I suggest to clients that we try such an exercise, I openly admit that I do not know why it works but that I have seen its good effects. As Patrick Casement said in an interview with Clare Pointon, 'I think there's a real skill in not having to know' (Casement, 2004, p. 12). I will leave the reader to explore that more fully, but the methods are there for use if wanted.

Caution

If we are working with a client who is barely in touch with reality, then fantasy work is not appropriate, and grounding types of activity, keeping firmly to reality and fact, should be used. In the section on suitability for therapy, which was examined in Chapter One, we noted that the client who is out of touch with reality is not a suitable candidate for therapy. From time to time, however, we may find ourselves, for example, in an intake session, with such a client and we need to take care to keep them as grounded as possible.

Gimmicks/techniques: cautionary note

It is important that different skills are used appropriately and seamlessly. It is also important to explain to the client the idea behind the technique. Skills are not used simply as gimmicks but to enable the client in some way.

Art work

For example, we may use art work where speech seems to be difficult or where a client simply cannot articulate what they are feeling. Drawing, painting, and the use of colour may enable the client both to convey what they want to the therapist and to actually release some of their pent-up feelings.

Relationships can be represented on paper, not great works of art, but symbolically to indicate how members of the family, for example, relate to each other. The colours chosen and where people are placed are the important factors, not artistic prowess.

In Rawson, 2002, pp. 211–220, Client 'I' was a gifted artist, but the drawings of her abuser, drawn in the heat of an emotional moment, are in stark contrast to the more controlled and sophisticated artwork of some of the other pictures. All of them are expressive but, I suspect, that the most therapeutic are those on pp. 215–216, which could be taken for the work of a young child. Art in therapy is about what helps.

Chair work

Introducing chair work, i.e., inviting the client to address the absent person by imagining them in a chair in the room, can be helpful. This idea needs to be explained, as far as we can, to the client. We, as therapists, may be familiar with the concept, but it is a rather strange idea for the client. Some will, indeed, find it impossible to do this kind of imaginary work, at least in front of the therapist. However, they may try it at home and find that it is useful.

Writing

It can be helpful to the client to write to the person whom they need to address. Then they have a record of what they have said and at times it seems almost as if the words take off and they are sometimes surprised at what they find themselves writing.

Tape recording

Some therapists record the sessions with their client and let the client take away the tape to listen to. As they then listen to the tape of the session the client is asked to make notes about points that strike them as significant in some way. These then can be discussed further with the therapist. If this is to be done, it is best to wait a few days after the recording before listening to the tape, so that one hears it better. You may have noticed that when you proof read, even a letter or short piece of writing, that if you read it after a few days you notice mistakes that you overlooked when reading it soon after writing it. It seems that a little distance makes for a certain clarity in such instances. Perhaps, certainly in the case of the tape, one's defences drop a little so that we find ouselves facing the reality.

Stones/buttons/interlocking Russian dolls

Some therapists will make use of different shaped stones to get a picture of the client's relationships. They ask the client to choose a stone for each person and to say why they have chosen that one. Then the client is asked to place each stone on the surface and to say why they are putting them where they do in relation one to the other. This can be a very powerful exercise and very revealing, and can help the client to articulate what is going on for them. It can enable the client to see more clearly what is happening in the family dynamic and it can continue to be used creatively as therapist and client explore the changes the client wishes to make. Buttons or other objects can be used to equally good effect. The different sizes and shapes give plenty of choice to the client as they remind them of significant others in their lives. The dolls that fit inside one another in different sizes can also be useful in this sort of exercise. I believe that they are commonly known as Russian dolls.

Goodbye letter

In *Grappling with Grief*, there are a number of suggestions of activities to help oneself or others, especially at times of grief (Rawson, 2004, Chapters Five and Six, pp. 73–106). Some of these can be adapted to fit other issues also.

One that come to mind is the idea of writing a good bye letter to a loved one (*ibid.* p.76).

Symbolically letting go

A dramatic and powerful symbolic action of letting go can be made using helium balloons. This might be thought about if one is ready to 'let go' of someone who has died or who is no longer in one's life through a divorce or a break-up of a relationship. It could equally be applied to something that is no longer available for us, such as a job or career or something that is no longer wanted in our life, like a bad habit. I would suggest that a nice place is found to release the balloon and that one takes time to reflect and think a little about both the good and the bad side of the situation that is being let go; the idea being to release one to get on with one's new life, enriched by the good that has been part of one's past life and unencumbered by the bad that may equally have been present. With regard to both the good and the bad, one hopes that lessons have been learned that will help us to enhance the good and avoid the bad as we continue life's journey.

Symbolic remembering

Another idea is that of symbolically remembering a deceased person, e.g., planting a bush or tree as a symbol. The actual planting can be a ceremonial act. It can be a way of putting a full stop and going on with life, a way of saying goodbye (Rawson, 2004).

Practice and supervision

I suggest that the therapist needs to have practised these various ideas, at least on themselves and ideally with other therapists. Appropriate supervision needs to be built in. The topic of supervision is returned to in a later chapter, but now we turn to the ending of therapy.

CHAPTER NINE

ENDINGS

In a one to one contract the last session would consist of some 'work' but also a review of what the client has learned, whether they have achieved what they wanted to, and what remains to be done.

The client can be helped to see what they have learned, including new skills that they can utilize in their day to day life.

Some of the questions that will be in the therapist's mind are as follows:

> Does their learning from the sessions correspond with what they had hoped to learn?
> Are there still things that they need to explore?

The client needs to come to a clear view as to what they would still like to learn.

> Do they need the therapist to help them with this or are they now better equipped to do it on their own?

Last session

The last session provides therapist and client with a fixed deadline and this puts a certain pressure on both not to waste any time. As in the short piece, which was seen in the quick reference notes entitled 'The dynamics of the deadline', we all know the effect of a cut-off date for essays, job applications, or a report for a board meeting. A deadline has a wonderful way of concentrating the mind. Many people seem unable to achieve results without a deadline to work to. Brief therapy clearly capitalizes on this.

Great achievements in little time, if that is all one has!

Therapists will be able to cite many examples of client work, which has miraculously speeded up when the client is emigrating, moving, ending term, or having to stop therapy for some other reason.

Joan: one session therapy

Once I had a student come to see me on the last day of term. She had walked out of an exam because she simply could not seem to do it. She was a good student and knew the material, but couldn't get on with the exam. She went to the station some forty minutes away in order to go home but, sitting there, she remembered that, at the student induction session a couple of years earlier, I had said, 'Before you pack your bags to go home come and see me'. So she turned around and came back. I made a space to see her. We explored the obvious possibilities for her block, such as, had she felt prepared for the paper?; did she want to pass?; did she like the course?, and all seemed positive. I asked what *exactly* had happened. Could she talk me through *exactly* what she had done and where it all went wrong. She had, in fact, gone quite normally into the exam room and started to look at the paper but 'It all seemed so pointless and unimportant . . .' she trailed off. As she spoke she had curled up in a ball, her head almost below her knees, in foetal position as far as sitting in a chair would allow. She was almost hidden behind her long, flowing hair. I became silent and waited, having noted the words 'pointless and unimportant'. After a bit I (P) asked:

'What is happening?'

She (J) said, 'I'm feeling so sad.' She maintained the same position.

P: 'Do you know what that is about?'

J: 'I'm thinking of my brother.'

P: 'Can you tell me?'

It transpired that her brother had committed suicide a few years earlier, just as she was doing a set of important exam papers, as she had been on this occasion. The family had never talked about what had happened, but had just pretended he had never existed and simply gone on with their lives. It had all seemed so unreal.

Joan had wanted to talk about what had happened, and what she felt, and the effect it had on all the family. The guilt, the questions, the anger and hurt. She had failed the last exam previously, and felt that she had not received the support and help she had needed at the time.

Joan had come to me on the last day of term en route for home to take up a holiday job literally hundreds of miles away. There was therefore no chance of continuing therapy at this time, so we had to get as far as possible in this one session. There seemed to be a clear link, which made sense to both of us, with the previous important exams and with these ones. It would seem that the latter was the trigger for the memory and the 'unfinished business' from the loss of her brother. Having talked and cried about her brother and the whole family situation and made the connection about the exam, we needed to decide what to do next. There were practicalities in terms of informing tutors and arranging resits, etc. She felt well able to sort these things. She wanted to feel free in the family to talk about the suicide and her brother. She wanted them to know how awful it was for her. She wanted them to acknowledge how bad it was for them, too. She hoped that they might all be able to share their loss, pain, and grief. I talked a little about loss and different reactions and suggested that, now she had managed to talk and experience her deep feelings about it all with me, perhaps she could be the one to open the subject with her parents. It was a very emotional session and I was a little concerned at the fact that she was going so far away from support, should she need it. I gave her the address of the British Association of Psychotherapy and Counselling, who could put her in touch with a counsellor/therapist in any part of the country should she need it, and offered her a telephone session if she needed it before the next term started.

I also suggested that she take a little time out before setting off home again and that I would be available if she wished to return before the end of the working day. However, I saw this as precautionary, rather than really expecting her to avail herself of it. I quote it as an example of flexibility. Two sessions in one day would be very unusual, but so were her circumstances and, as it happened, I had the space that day. The offer of a telephone session is also an example of flexibility and appropriate in this particular circumstance. The very fact that she was given the opportunity to do this would in itself be a support. I did not actually anticipate that she would do so.

By chance, I crossed paths with Joan at the start of the following term, and she approached me in the corridor. I barely recognized this confident, self-possessed looking student. She had gone home later that day and had tackled her parents about her brother's death, how he died, how awful it all had been, how she had been so affected, especially by the secrecy and ignoring of the whole situation. She found that they, too, were glad to talk and that they had all shared a great deal over the holidays. This had resulted in the family situation being very much improved. She had also organized her resit, talked to the tutors, taken and passed the exam and was raring to go for the new term.

The one session had indeed helped. A real case of the client becoming not just her own therapist but that of the family too!

Loss for the client

It is not just the client who can feel loss at the end of a therapy contract, it can also be a loss for the therapist. First, though, I will look at loss for the client.

End of therapy as a step forward

One hopes that the end of therapy is seen as a step forward, as a moving on in a positive way. Some will be glad to regain the time that they have given up for therapy, and will be quite pleased to move on from looking at painful areas. At times, because of what has been shared, the client who is ready to move on will be glad that they can leave behind the therapist and that part of their lives that they have shared. It is as if they are starting over. There may also be sadness at moving on and never seeing the therapist again, since a lot will have been shared. Surely these reactions are natural. The therapist has been there as a dependable person and, at times, as a real life-line and someone entrusted with deep secrets.

Defence mechanisms or unfinished business

For some there will be defence mechanisms against the forthcoming loss and comments such as 'It was no good anyway' can come into play. Not owning that anything has changed or that what has taken place in therapy has helped, is another ruse. Here the therapist can remind clients of things that have changed, as they probably will have, and remind them of some examples of things that do seem different now. Sometimes the original problem rears its head again. Again the therapist helps the client to see how the original problem is not quite the same now.

These may be simply defence mechanisms and, as they are explored with the client, they dissipate, and the client acknowledges that indeed change has occurred and that they are ready to go it alone.

However, the client's reluctance to end may also indicate that there is some unfinished business, and this needs to be addressed before the client can leave therapy in a positive way. A new brief contract might be required to conclude the work, or this may be very quickly dealt with in the remaining time available within the existing contract. This will be jointly negotiated, as has been highlighted elsewhere. The brief therapist perhaps needs to ask themselves if they have kept the client to the agreed focus as well as they could have. It may be that the originally agreed focus has been allowed to go out of focus a little, and that this is the reason for the unfinished business.

As the end of the sessions are nearing, other issues of loss may emerge for the client, triggered by the end of therapy. For example, on rare occasions the client may feel rejected or abandoned. In this situation it may be that a separate endings contract may be required. One hopes, however, that these feelings would have emerged in the first session; for example, with a client who resists the idea of a short contract. In exploring such a client's fears that a few sessions may not be enough, earlier losses may have been revealed; these need to be addressed. I would anticipate that these would be bound up with what the client wants to address in therapy. In this case they would become part of the initial contract.

Shift back to equality

In therapy or as a student, we allow ourselves to depend somewhat on the therapist or tutor. Towards the end of a therapy contract one often notices a sort of equalizing that occurs. Many therapists will recognize the slight shift that takes place between client and therapist as they near the end of their contract, where there seems to be a more equalizing aspect within the relationship. Often this is indicated by a small thing such as the client recognizing that one might be looking tired, or the client might comment on a change in the room, or ask where one is going on holiday. Whereas in the early days of a contract the therapist might bat such a comment back, querying why the question was important, now they might simply answer the question or acknowledge the comment. In the earlier part of the contract the client is often too absorbed in their issues to be able to notice anything outside of that. Or, on the other hand, they might be using a more personal comment as a way of avoiding their issues.

Loss for the therapist

For the therapist, too, there can be loss. The therapist, for a brief period, has been intensely involved in the client's story. The therapist needs to be able to let go, to encourage the client to go it alone and to trust that they can. In the phrase 'teaching the client to become their own therapist' we are, in effect, giving away our skills and teaching them to do without us. The therapist needs to maintain a certain detachment at all times; despite the involvement referred to earlier it is a detached involvement.

Respect for and trust in the client's ability to cope

The therapist, therefore, needs to have a great deal of respect for the other person's ability to cope and to trust this. As therapists, we are both teacher and facilitator. This perhaps demands a certain humility on the part of therapists, as they acknowledge that they are not indispensable. The therapist needs to be flexibile, to allow for more sessions later, if that is what is required. A good parent has to allow the child to move away, but is always there in the background. The doctor deals with the presenting issue, but is still available if the patient returns with another unconnected, or related issue. The therapist, at times, can see areas that perhaps the client could benefit from work-ing on, and these might be voiced, but it is not the ther-apist's business to lead the way, that is the client's task. When the time is right, if they have had a good initial experience of therapy, then they will not hesitate to take it up again, if it is needed.

Ripple effect in therapy

There is a ripple effect in therapy. When one issue is resolved it tends to have a knock-on effect on other areas of a person's life. (See *Parables*, Rawson, 1990.)

Demanding on the therapist

The quick succession of clients with the very intense and deep work of brief therapy is very demanding for the ther-apist. The therapist has to be very ready to let go of their clients. This sort of work is very stimulating, challenging, and rewarding but, pleased as we must be at their progress, there is a loss as the client with whom we have worked moves on. We rarely get to hear of the long-term outcome, since we are but a small part of the client's jour-ney and one that they may be pleased to leave well behind with its associated painful memories. It can feel, as for client 'I' almost as if the client is a stranger to the person they now are. Client 'I' read what I had written about our work together and said:

> After reading the report my mind began to remember how I felt during those sessions and this seemed so far removed from what I feel today. I realised that I was justified in being so angry and that I used this anger to shield the pain. When reading this there was no pain, no anger, only

sadness about this 'stranger's' childhood and the solace she sought in drink and drugs. [Rawson, 2002, p. 228]

Review

As we have seen above, in the last session of therapy we review with the client what has been covered and what needs to be covered further. In the next chapter I undertake a similar exercise with regard to this book.

QUICK REFERENCE NOTES

Coping with loss: the end from the beginning

- Setting the expectation from session one that there is an end in view. e.g., 'Let's look at *x* for *y* sessions, then we'll review and see if we've achieved what you've come for'.

or

'I normally work in a focused way for *x–y* sessions with people and usually they're able to cope on their own after that . . .'

- Introducing the client to the idea of helping themselves by thinking between sessions. 'This way it speeds up the process'
- Dealing with the 'it doesn't seem long enough' queries from clients, e.g., 'Are there other situations in your experience where you didn't feel you had enough? What was it you wanted from (parent or whoever)?'– this may then become the focus of the sessions and will probably relate to the presenting problem.
  (Transference is there from session one. The 'it's not enough'exploration is also dealing with the resistance.)
- The countdown of sessions serves as an ongoing reminder of the pending end – the loss and also the deadline effect impact, e.g., 'We've two more sessions and then the review'.
- The penultimate session is often the key session
- Exploration of feelings about the end; this needs to be flagged up prior to the review session.

Loss for the client

The client is attached to the therapist as a:

- lifeline;
- listener;
- dependable person;
- trusted person;
- person who has been entrusted with the client's deep secrets and inner world, hence the loss of the therapist can be painful.

Hoped for reactions

That the loss of the therapist will be seen:

- as good;
- as a mark of progress, change and moving on;
- as a relief that the painful exploration to reach this stage is now over;
- as appropriate, since the therapy relationship is an unreal, one-sided relationship;
- as appropriately sad, since the therapy relationship is an intense and special relationship dealing with very deep issues.

The following ordinary reactions to loss and grief, if present, would point to some unfinished business or premature ending

- Feeling bereft.
- Feeling deserted.
- Feeling left.
- Feeling rejected.

- Feeling isolated.
- Overwhelming sadness.

Ordinary defence mechanisms can come into play, also pointing to unfinished business

- denial;
- rubbishing, e.g., 'no good anyway';
- re-emergence of presenting problem;
- not owning the importance of the sessions/changes that have occurred.

Loss for the therapist in short-term work

- Loss because of
  - intensity of therapeutic relationship – deep but brief;
  - constant turnover of clients.
  This is very demanding for the therapist.

- It challenges the therapist's ability:
  - to let go of the client;
  - to encourage growth and independence;
  - to trust that change can happen without him/her;
  - to keep to the contract;
  - to be flexible in negotiating a new contract;
  - to ignore therapeutic detours;
  - to give away expertise.

- It requires of the therapist the attitude of:
  - a teacher;
  - a facilitator;
  - optimism;
  - respect for the person's ability to cope;
  - trust in the person's ability to cope;
  - availability – e.g., the therapist can be there if more sessions are required later. Similar to the way parents are in the background as children grow up and lead their own lives;
  - flexibility, open to new contract or review sessions or staggered sessions.

Homework

Be more aware of the following ideas:

- Client as own therapist.
- Giving the client the tools.
- Focusing.
- What is the contract?
- The end from the beginning.
- Issues of loss for client and the therapist.
- The dynamics of the deadline.

CHAPTER TEN

REVIEW AND WHAT NEXT?

What has been covered?

In these pages I have encompassed the material that would normally be presented in a three-day course to give practising therapists a working idea of the basics of brief psychodynamic psychotherapy. I have briefly covered all the points in the following summary, which is repeated in the quick reference notes at the end of the concluding chapter for the reader's convenience as a final summary.

Brief psychodynamic psychotherapy

Summary of the basics
The contract

PRE-REQUISITES FOR BEST RESULTS

Experience required of the therapist
Motivation on the part of the client

Key principles of brief psychodynamic psychotherapy

1. Understanding of psychodynamic principles.
2. Importance of the first session.

3. Therapy as short as client need allows.
4. Early establishment of the therapeutic alliance.
5. Therapist attitude.
6. Teaching.
7. Enabling clients to become their own therapists.
8. Activity.
9. Focus.
10. Flexibility and fusion.
11. Incisiveness.

Principle of principles and key permeating feature

12. The sensitivity of the therapist in order to be in tune with the client.

HOPED FOR CONSEQUENCES WITHIN SESSIONS

Hope >> Involvement >> Intensity >> Magic

HOPED FOR CONSEQUENCES AS A RESULT OF THERAPY

1. Client is capable of being own therapist
2. Client is free from past to cope with present

A new slant

I suggest that it is the *early application of an appropriate combination* of the above that is a contributing factor in the shortening of therapy. All of the key facets need to be held in mind simultaneously.

This outline of the basics is an abbreviated version of the conceptual framework that I formulated as the culmination of several years of academic work based on practice. Those of you who wish to know how I arrived at the conceptual framework, or to read the fuller version need to turn to *Short Term Psychodynamic Psychotherapy: An Analysis of Key Principles* (Rawson, 2002). There I have detailed the lengthy research which led to this and provide a more in depth exposition of the principles.

Sensitivity; incisiveness; involvement; intensity; magic

Before ending, there are some points to which I want to draw especial attention. These are: 'sensitivity' and 'incisiveness', 'involvement', 'intensity', and 'magic'. These aspects of short-term therapy have been implied, inferred, or referred to on and off throughout the book. They are very special.

Magic

The magic that I mention is hard to describe, but therapist and client will, I think, recognize those moments of 'insight', 'awareness', 'being', to use a word from Martin Buber, or 'change', that defy description but definitely happen.

Intensity, involvement and incisiveness

There is something about the intensity and involvement of both client and therapist that contributes to the magic referred to above. To facilitate change quickly requires a certain incisiveness on the part of the therapist. I believe that this is possible, in the brief time, because of the intense involvement of client and therapist. This, in turn, only happens because of the sensitivity of the therapist and the 'attunement' of the therapist to their client.

Sensitivity

I refer to sensitivity as 'the Principle of Principles and the Key Permeating Feature of the Short term Psychodynamic Psychotherapy approach: The sensitivity of the therapist in order to be in tune with the client' (Rawson, 2002 p. 270).

Next step

The best next step for students wanting to take their learning further in brief therapy is, in my view, to find a supervisor skilled in the method, either individually or within a group. If there is a group training supervision, where role playing and practice of exercises is possible, this would be very good. There is no reason why this cannot be supervision that would count towards any requirement for professional and accreditation purposes. Different professional bodies have various requirements for supervision and these are complex for group supervision. Therefore, group members need to ensure that the time allowed for supervision meets the requirement of their particular professional body.

The question of supervision

To work in this brief way, I suspect, does require that one has a supervisor who is familiar with it, or at least sympathetic to it. It may be, however, that one has to change supervisors to find one who helps. Some therapists have begun to work in the brief method and have come up against adverse comments from their supervisor. This is a problem. It is important to see what was happening in the therapeutic setting and what specifically was the supervisor's objection. However, mostly in these situations it would seem to be an ideological objection rather than one that, as a brief therapy advocate, I could agree with.

I sympathize with students or therapists in this position. I myself trained in the long-term analytical work and in the short-term simultaneously. I had different supervisors in each setting. Each setting expected a different way of working and one had to follow what was required within each. However, thankfully, once one is no longer a student, to be assessed in a certain way of working, one is free to choose from the good that one has learned on one's journey and fuse these to the best effect for our clients. In my case, as I was training in long- and short-term psychodynamic work simultaneously, I observed clients coming with similar issues to the long-term centre and to the short-term centre. In the first centre clients left after perhaps forty or fifty sessions, and in the short-term centre after eight. It seemed to me that if similar clients and issues could be dealt with quickly, then that was to be preferred. This led to my interest and research in the brief model. I have now moved on from the rigid eight sessions. I now advocate, as already stated, a more flexible approach: as many sessions as the client needs. This, as we saw earlier, tends to be around four to six sessions. Once out of the student milieu, just as we can choose how we work, we can usually also choose our supervisors. In some workplaces, however, that is not so, and this presents another difficulty, but not perhaps particular just to brief therapy. It is, perhaps, more for the therapist then to seek help from their professional organization, or maybe to seek a situation compatible with their own ideals. Incidentally, if a therapist really does not wish to work in the brief way and if this goes against the grain for them, I question whether it is really wise for them to work in this way at all.

Supervision: how much?

There is ongoing debate in the profession about supervision in general and for brief therapy in particular, and my responses to some of the opinions that have been published appear below in the quick reference notes (pp. 177–185).

Brief therapy for the twenty-first century

There is also in the quick reference notes that follow, a copy of an article entitled 'Brief therapy for the twenty first century', which seems an appropriate summary as we near the end of this book (pp. 174–176).

QUICK REFERENCE NOTES

Letter to the editor BACP journal *Counselling* (Rawson 1999a, p. 181), as part of debate on how much supervision and whether brief therapy is good or bad

Dear Editor,

Brief Therapy

I recently enjoyed reading Dr Gertrude Mander's honest grapplings with some of the important issues around the supervision of brief therapists and her ensuing struggle with the concept that 'short can be good' (1998). Equally Dr Brian Thorne's most readable exploration of brief therapy as 'good or bad' (1999).

I have practised the brief approach for more than twenty years, and supervise and train in the approach. The two articles drew my attention and prompted the following response.

Dr Mander's article raised some questions for me. Her expectation for example of intensive supervision, i.e. three sessions for a case of five sessions, seems puzzling. I would endorse such intensive supervision *only* in the case of a trainee therapist or as a training supervision for a therapist learning brief work or for a particularly difficult case or where the therapist is grappling with their own transferential issues and needs much guidance with these. Apart from these instances surely one supervision session might be enough unless a specific issue is raised or needs to be raised by the supervisor. Many people seeing clients for brief contracts may have say sixteen to twenty clients per week. It is not possible that every one is going to be brought to supervision in the way she recommends. In looking at casework there are common issues and themes and the scrutiny of one case may well move along others also. Of course any special problem that the therapist may be having with a client may mean that a case will need more than one visit and might even be reviewed every supervision. One of the key principles emerging from my research about brief therapy was that of flexibility. This related to both time and techniques. I would also recommend appropriate flexibility for therapist and supervisor. Additionally I am one of the school of thought that believes that each supervisee in a group benefits from the supervision of other supervisee's cases and I have long questioned BAC's way of calculating the 'individual equivalent' time of supervision for those who attend group supervision.

One or two other aspects of her article drew my attention and an alternative viewpoint.

Her student counselling supervisees with unappreciative management, and student clients who have difficulty engaging in the process of counselling, demonstrate only one side of the coin.

The student Counselling Service I managed found that students readily contracted for flexible short-term contracts, attended the sessions with great commitment and seemed to reach satisfyingly positive results. Brian Thorne's article refers to my experience of committed student clients too! Also was I exceptionally lucky to have had appreciative management for most of my early career as a College Counsellor in the Higher Education sector?

Her suggesting to her supervisee that staff counselling should be referred elsewhere is, I suggest, an over simplification. Many colleges have built into the counsellors' contracts that they see staff for counselling as well as students. So the boundary issues in this regard have to be managed and cannot simply be avoided by referral elsewhere.

Another disturbing point mentioned in passing by Mander is that some people apparently liken brief therapy to a 'death experience'. Despite having spent the last few years researching about brief dynamic psychotherapy, this is a new one on me. For whom is it a death experience? The therapist? What is this saying? Is it a reference to the detached involvement required of any therapist? Is it about the quick turn over of clients and the need for the therapist to be able to 'let go' of the client, which is certainly necessary and requires an ability to sustain loss? Does it refer to the satisfying outcome of the client moving onwards more freely, or leaving their pain behind, or having come to terms with an inevitable situation or excitedly going forward to a new phase of life? I suppose one could liken these positive results to a resurrection experience?

Returning to Dr Thorne's article, I believe the power and intensity of the encounter that he describes, in his Brief Person-Centred experiments, captures the essence of what takes place in brief therapy sessions. In my recent empirical research analysing the key principles of brief psychodynamic psychotherapy, the intensity and involvement, which happens consistently within brief therapy sessions, emerged as very important aspects of the process. I do hope this later scepticism dissipates and his original joy at the involvement and speed of progress reasserts itself. So that he dares to spread the 'heresy' of Person – Centred Brief Therapy further.

By the way what therapy is not centred on the person?

Yours sincerely,

Penny Rawson (Dr)

Supervision nonsense (Rawson, 2003)

I am writing in response to Alan Pickett's letter about the number of supervision hours (CPJ October 2002). The hours for supervision were decided almost 20 years ago. How do I know? I was (dare I say it?) there. The decision was made at a time when the whole accreditation system needed to be tightened up. I hope that the accreditation revisions contributed to the raising of standards. However, I believe that the time has come to bring this supervision requirement up to date. In this I am thinking particularly about senior counsellors – how one defines that this is a matter of debate. Perhaps by number of client hours seen overall?

Many counsellors see fewer clients per week as they get more involved in supervision, training, writing etc. Since the minimum hours of counselling per year has been relaxed some may see a client just now and then and maybe not weekly. If, for example, a counsellor sees a client for two hours in a month, there is then a nonsensical requirement that in that same month the counsellor must have one hour and a half hours [*sic*] of supervision. A full-time therapist might see 20 clients a week (80 sessions a month) and still be required to have the same amount of supervision. Having been at both ends of the spectrum I question this. Even economically it is nonsensical. If one saw a client for just one session in a month for say £40, one would then require supervision at say £60 per month i.e. counselling at a loss. It is time for a review.

Alan Pickett suggested a proportional idea e.g. one hour's supervision for every 10 hours of counselling. I would support this idea if we have to have a rule. However I would prefer a system which allowed senior counsellors to seek supervision as and when they felt it to be necessary.

Therapy for the 21st century (Rawson, 1999b)

The fact that this issue of *Counselling News* is dedicated to the topic of brief therapy in itself shows a radical development in the public and professional awareness of this approach. Such an event would not have happened earlier. For some inexplicable reason, the secret of short-term therapy seems to get lost time and time again over the year. It is not new and yet is currently in the throes of being discovered anew. I hope that this article evolving from my research will help to reinforce brief therapy's place on the map and its development onwards as we reach the turn of the century.

I hope to kindle readers' interest to know more, to raise questions as familiar techniques are referred to here in the context of unfamiliar brevity. I hope to challenge those who say this short-term approach cannot achieve good results, with authentic client comments that defy this assumption. I also aim to encourage those who practise brief therapy reluctantly, because their employers say they must or because clients can afford no more sessions, and who strive to help but dare not believe this is possible in a few sessions.

What do we mean by short-term?

There are many interpretations as to what 'short' means in the context of therapy. The time scale that I am referring to is flexible and is negotiated with the client according to individual need. A case may take one session, the more usual number required ranges between four and six sessions, and sometimes more. Twelve would be considered one of the long cases.

From statistics of many college counselling services, for example, it is clear that many cases consist of one session only. These, I would suggest, do not denote failure or imply that it is simply skimming the surface. The client has simply got what they needed at that time.

In a college service that I managed, the average over a year was four sessions. In an EAP (Employee Assistance Programme) with which I was recently involved, where the number of sessions was negotiated quite freely, the average over a year was 5.5 sessions.

The question is not *how long have we got?* It is *what do we do with the time we have?*

A joint enterprise

I use the term 'we' above advisedly, since short-term therapy is a joint enterprise and one in which the time and the subject matter to be worked on is negotiated.

I have already referred to a negotiated timescale. If the timescale is to be short, the therapist's attitude is all-important. If the therapist believes in the method, they will convey this confidence to the client, who very often in fact only expected one or two sessions anyway. Some clients however, do think therapy has to be a very long process and if the therapist secretly or openly believes that this is so, then the therapy is likely to be protracted. It is here, especially, that the therapist's *genuine belief* in the process of short-term therapy is important. This, coupled with the natural effect of what I call the *dynamics of the deadline*, set a promising course for a successful brief therapy contract.

The history

The idea of therapy being short is not a new one, although

it seems as if the concept has to be repeatedly rediscovered. Many of Freud's successors were unhappy with the time that analysis seemed to take and began to experiment with different techniques to shorten the process.

Ferenczi in the 1920s thought that passivity in the therapist caused 'the stagnation of analysis' and began to be far more active in an attempt to speed things along. Rank, in the 1940s, emphasised the need for the therapist to mobilise the client's will in order to shorten therapy, and introduced time limits. Alexander, also in the 1940s, recommended gaps in therapy or 'interruptions' which encouraged clients to stand on their own feet and discouraged dependence. This idea fits well with normal human development, with its spurts of growth and then latent periods in which the individual digests what has been learned, and experiments a little with the newfound knowledge. Alexander also stressed the importance of being flexible enough to adapt the technique to the needs of the patient. He experimented with the use of the couch and chair, with timescales, and with the control and manipulation of the transference. The ideas represented by these early pioneers of the brief approach were considered daring modifications at that time, but are considered normal for the brief therapist working in the late 1990s.

Psychodynamic

Readers will notice the reference above to transference and yes, brief therapy can be psychodynamic. There are now many forms of therapy which are brief in duration, some of the better known being Solution Focused Therapy and Cognitive Analytic Therapy, but from my recent research, there emerged 15 other titles also! It seems, as Gustafson suggests, that the proponents of each approach were 'ambitious . . . to define a standard technique of their own'. He suggests that they then become 'defenders of their own dogma'. Are these approaches really so different or can each learn the best from the other? I prefer to see a fusion of ideas with the client's need to the forefront. These may be from other branches of brief therapy, and other traditions within the therapeutic world.

This article refers to Short Term Psychodynamic Psychotherapy. (The terms psychotherapy and psychodynamic counselling are used interchangeably.) It incorporates the concepts of transference and it works with the past. As Louis Marteau observes, we need to be 'reaching through to the very root' if any change is to occur. Thus, the brief work is in no way superficial, it is not palliative but anticipates real change. Malan in the 1960s would have referred to this as working at the 'radical' end of the spectrum.

Client comments

In my own practice, it has led to client comments at the end of therapy such as: 'I am free'; 'I feel as if I'm waking up after a long sleep'; 'I can cope alone now'; 'After reading the report, my mind began to remember how I felt during those sessions and this seemed so far removed from what I feel today. I realised I was justified in being so angry and that I had used the anger to shield the pain. When reading this there was no pain, no anger, only sadness about this 'stranger's' childhood and the solace she sought in drink and drugs.'

The focus

By the 1960s, it was widely agreed that for brief therapy,

a focus is important. Sifneos is particularly noted for his reference to circumscribing the focus and for seeing it as a joint venture, which I fully endorse. However, I want to stress that although client and therapist choose to put the spotlight on the strategic focus in a person's life, this does not mean that the one aspect is examined in isolation. In dealing with the one issue, there is a ripple effect and this one issue also affects other aspects of the individual's life. As human beings, it is really not possible to isolate one aspect of ourselves. If, for example, we have a toothache, does it not dominate our whole being? Is not an emotional ache equally pervasive? It is, of course, true that just as a pain-killer may help the physical ache, so we devise all sorts of ways of numbing the emotional, too – not always helpful ways. The flexible techniques alluded to earlier help to uncover some of these devices so that the ache can be dealt with and healing can take place, freeing the person to move forward.

The first session

The focus needs to be found early on, preferably in the first session, and as we note the need for speed in finding the focus, the need for activity and flexibility on the therapist's part also becomes apparent. I believe that the first session is of paramount importance. There are a number of features in the first session that I would wish to draw attention to, but it is perhaps the testing out of the therapist that needs to be highlighted, especially since it is more usual to hear about the therapist assessing the client. I suggest that it is important that the therapist passes the client's test. That is: 'Is this person able to understand me? Can they bear my pain? Can they pick up the clues I give?'

To recap, there is the need to focus, to be active, to be flexible and to take especial note of all that takes place in the first session, especially in acknowledging the pain. Despite being rooted in the analytic tradition, even the early brief therapists, who were mostly trained analysts, actively embraced techniques from other traditions. Wolberg in the 60s, for example, referring to a 'fusion of skills'. Is he the precursor of the modern trend for integration of post 'schoolism', as Clarkson terms it. Certainly, anyone wanting to work briefly could do well to examine his exposition of the brief approach, which has much to teach us today.

Some of the methods I find especially useful involve gestalt techniques, fantasy work and the client doing work in between sessions on their own. This might involve reflecting on the work within the session, or perhaps looking up key dates in their history or undertaking some relevant task. All the above involve the client and I suspect that it is the client involvement that is the key to success. As Van Kaan says: 'To be there means that I gather together all my thoughts, feelings and memories. I am wholly with what I am doing, creating, perceiving.'

Special demands on the therapist

This being so, there is also a particular sort of involvement required of the therapist in working briefly with the clients. This can sometimes be difficult for the therapist. There is an intense relationship for just a short while and then the ending comes, a constant turnover that makes demands on the therapist who has to be prepared to let go and to sustain loss.

If the practitioner is in private practice, they also have to trust that new clients will come thick and fast as word gets round that they can be helped out of pain in a few sessions for a limited amount of money. Where therapy is offered free within, for example, EAPs, there is certainly no shortage of clients and there is a good success rate in the short number of sessions normally allowed.

Special rewards for the brief therapist

The rapidity with which clients move on from their presenting problems to go it alone with confidence is greatly rewarding. It also serves as a reminder of the resilience of the human being and the privilege we have, in participating briefly but deeply, in the lives of those who choose to come to us.

Bibliography

Clarkson, P. (1998). Beyond schoolism – the implications of psychotherapy outcome research for counselling and psychotherapy trainees. *Counsellor and Psychotherapist Dialogue 1*, *1*(2): 13–19.

Gustafson, J. P. (1986). *The Complex Secret of Brief Psychotherapy*. New York: W. W. Norton.

Marteau, L. (1986). *Existential Short Term Therapy*. London: The Dympna Centre.

Rawson, P. (1990). *Parables*. London: FASTPACE.

Rawson, P. (1992). Focal and short-term therapy is a treatment of choice. *Counselling*, *5*: 106–107.

Rawson, P. (1995). By mutual arrangement. *Counselling News*, *6*: 8–9.

Van Kaan, A., (1970). *On Being Involved. The Rhythm of Involvement and Detachment in Daily Life*. Denville, NJ: Dimension Books

Wolberg, L (Ed.) (1965). *The Technique of Short Term Psychotherapy*. New York: Grune and Stratton.

CHAPTER ELEVEN

CONCLUSION

To conclude, then, I have presented the reader with a basic guide as to the key concepts in the practice of brief psychodynamic psychotherapy. This is a brief psychodynamic method that deals with the past through the present, in order to improve the present and future. It is not a superficial, sticking plaster approach. I have not laboured aspects of transference or countertransference, nor other basic aspects of therapy in general, since these are part of the knowledge I would expect of the experienced therapist. Rather, I stress aspects such as activity, flexibility, and the fusion of skills, an agreed focus and time span for the work, and the importance of the first session, all of which can enable the work to move on more swiftly. These aspects were stressed in turn by the earlier proponents of the brief method. One recalls that most of the early proponents were analysts, so the stress on these aspects was really very innovative. In the above pages I have attempted to highlight the key issues and to demonstrate how these ideas can be incorporated into the brief work in practice.

I hope that this book may whet the reader's appetite and encourage therapists to incorporate some of the ideas into their work in brief therapy. Some may be tempted to read my earlier study that has been referred to from time to time in this book: *Short-Term Psychodynamic*

Psychotherapy: An Analysis of Key Principles. This gives a more in depth exposition, based on several years of research.

I have provided here an easily accessible outline of the basics of the approach. One of my aims is to make the brief method of therapy better known and understood. In therapy, people reveal areas of pain in their lives to the therapist. Facilitated by the therapist, they then work with and through these areas of pain to a more free existence. Brief therapy can accelerate that process. My advocacy of the method is to do with the economy of pain, not of money.

One day I would like to see centres available everywhere, where people could access short-term psychodynamic therapy, independently and for free. This would, no doubt, require government funding to achieve, but in terms of money lost to the country because of emotional and psychological problems this concept would, I think, prove fiscally economic. I hope that this book will contribute in some small way towards these objectives.

I will end with a repeat of the summary of the basics, referred to in the previous chapter, which provides a clear and simple guide to the basics of the method.

BRIEF PSYCHODYNAMIC PSYCHOTHERAPY: SUMMARY OF THE BASICS

The contract

Experience required of the therapist
Motivation on the part of the client

Key principles of brief psychodynamic psychotherapy

1. Understanding of psychodynamic principles.
2. Importance of the first session.
3. Therapy as short as client need allows.
4. Early establishment of the therapeutic alliance.
5. Therapist attitude.
6. Teaching.
7. Enabling clients to become their own therapists.
8. Activity.
9. Focus.
10. Flexibility and fusion.
11. Incisiveness.

Principle of principles and key permeating feature

12. The sensitivity of the therapist in order to be in tune with the client.

HOPED FOR CONSEQUENCES WITHIN SESSIONS

Hope >> Involvement >> Intensity >> Magic

HOPED FOR CONSEQUENCES AS A RESULT OF THERAPY

1. Client is capable of being own therapist
2. Client is free from past to cope with present

A new slant

I suggest that it is the *early application of an appropriate combination* of the above that is a contributing factor in the shortening of therapy. All of the key facets need to be held in mind simultaneously.

REFERENCES AND BIBLIOGRAPHY

Balint, M., Ornstein, P., & Balint, E. (1972). *Focal Psychotherapy: An Example of Applied Psychoanalysis*. London: Tavistock.

Casement, P. (2004). Learning from our mistakes. *Counselling and Psychotherapy Journal, 15*(06): 11–16.

de Shazer, S. (1990). What is it about brief therapy that works? In: J. Zeig & S. Gilligan (Eds.), *Brief Therapy, Myths, Methods and Metaphors*. New York: Brunner/Mazel.

Feltham, C. (1997). Challenging the core theoretical model. *Counselling, 5*: 121–125.

Feltham, C. (1997). *Time Limited Counselling*. London: Sage.

Goulding McClure, M. (1990). Getting the important work done fast. contract plus redecision. In: J. Zeig & S. Gilligan, (Eds.), *Brief Therapy, Myths, Methods and Metaphors*. New York: Brunner/Mazel.

Groves, J. (1992). The Short Term Dynamic Psychotherapies: An Overview in Psychotherapy for the 1990s. J. S. Rutan, (Ed.) London: The Guilford Press.

McGannon, M. (1996). *Staying Healthy, Fit and Sane in the Business Jungle*. London: Pitman.

Malan, D. (1963). *A Study of Brief Psychotherapy*. London: Tavistock Publications.

Malan, D. (1976). *The Frontier of Brief Psychotherapy, An Example of the Convergence of Research and Practice*, New York: Plenum Medical Books.

Mann, J. (1973). *Time Limited Psychotherapy*. MA: Harvard University Press.

Marteau, L. (1986). *Existential Short Term Therapy*. London: The Dympna Centre.

Molnos, A. (1987). Notes on selection of patients for dynamic brief psychotherapy (unpublished). Personal communication.

Molnos, A. (1995). *A Question of Time, Essentials of Brief Psychotherapy*. London: Karnac.

Rawson, P. (1990). *Parables*. London: FASTPACE.

Rawson, P. (1992). Focal and short-term therapy is a treatment of choice. *Counselling*, 5: 106–107.

Rawson, Penny, (1995), By mutual arrangement. *Counselling News*, 6: 8–9.

Rawson, Penny (1999a) Letters to the editor: 'Brief therapy'. *Counselling*, Aug: 181.

Rawson, P. (1999b) Therapy for the 21st century. *Counselling News*, March: 32–33.

Rawson, P. (2003). Supervision nonsense. *Counselling and Psychotherapy Journal*, February: Letters.

Rawson, P. (2002). *Short Term Psychodynamic Psychotherapy: An Analysis of Key Principles*. London: Karnac.

Rawson, P. (2004). *Grappling with Grief*. London: Karnac.

Sifneos, P. (1981). Short term anxiety provoking psychotherapy. Its history, technique, outcome and instruction. In: S.Budman (Ed.), *Forms of Brief Therapy*. New York: Guilford Press.

Sifneos, P. (1987). *Short Term Dynamic Psychotherapy Evaluation and Technique*. New York: Plenum Medical Books.

Wolberg, L. (Ed.) (1965). *The Technique of Short Term Psychotherapy*. New York: Grune and Stratton.

Yalom, I. (1931). *Existential Psychotherapy*. USA: Harper Collins [reprinted London: Basic Books, 1980].

INDEX